Fairness in Taxation

Exploring the Principles

Fairness in Taxation

Exploring the Principles

JOHN G. HEAD

LARS OSBERG

LESLIE GREEN

A. MARGUERITE CASSIN

LEO PANITCH

edited by

ALLAN M. MASLOVE

Published by University of Toronto Press in cooperation with the
Fair Tax Commission of the Government of Ontario

UNIVERSITY OF TORONTO PRESS
Toronto Buffalo London

Printed in Canada

ISBN 0-8020-7459-6

Printed on recycled paper

Canadian Cataloguing in Publication Data

Main entry under title:
Fairness in taxation : exploring the principles

"Published ... in cooperation with the Fair Tax Commission, Government of Ontario".
Includes bibliographical references.
ISBN 0-8020-7459-6

1. Tax incidence — Ontario. 2. Tax incidence.
3. Income tax — Ontario. I. Maslove, Allan M.,
1946–   . II. Ontario Fair Tax Commission.

HJ2323.C2F3 1993   336.2'94'09713   C92-095725-0

Contents

Foreword

The Ontario Fair Tax Commission was established to examine the province's tax system as an integrated whole and, in conjunction with its working groups, to analyse individual components of the system in detail.

It has been many years since the Ontario tax system was subjected to a comprehensive examination. However, a great deal of research on taxation has been undertaken over the past two decades. This work, based in several disciplines, has been both theoretical and applied, and in this context the research program of the Fair Tax Commission was formulated.

The research program has two broad purposes. The first is, of course, to support the deliberations of the commissioners. The second, more novel objective is to inform public discussions of tax matters so that the commission's formal and informal public consultations can be of maximum value. For this reason we have opted to publish volumes in the series of studies as they are ready, rather than holding them all until the commission has completed its work. While our approach is more difficult from a technical and administrative perspective, we believe that the benefits will justify our decision.

The research program seeks to synthesize the existing published work on taxation; to investigate the implications for Ontario of the general research work; and, where required, to conduct original research on the context and principles for tax reform and on specific tax questions. We thus hope to add to the existing body of knowledge without duplicating it. The studies included in these publications are those that we believe make a contribution to the literature on taxation.

I would like to extend my thanks to my fellow commissioners and to the members of the FTC secretariat. I also thank the many members of the working groups and the advisory groups who have contributed to the research program and to the overall work of the commission.

Monica Townson, Chair

Introduction

Many people's first reaction to the name "Fair Tax Commission" is that it is oxymoronic; there is no such thing as a fair tax. Flippancy aside, the comment reflects a view that fairness is "in the eye of the beholder" and that there are no widely accepted fairness principles on which to base tax systems (or other policy decisions). Is this commonly held perception correct?

To explore the idea of fairness and its relationship to the design of tax systems, the Fair Tax Commission invited five distinguished scholars to contribute papers. Professor John Head was asked to provide a "state of the art" discussion of fairness as it is currently reflected in economics, particularly in the public-finance literature. In addition, A. Marguerite Cassin, Leslie Green, Lars Osberg, and Leo Panitch were requested to explore, from their respective disciplines and perspectives, additional dimensions of fairness. Earlier drafts of the latter four papers were presented and discussed at a seminar organized by the commission.

John Head's survey and evaluation of the economics literature is presented from the viewpoint of one of the leading exponents of the Haig-Simons approach to equitable taxation. Notwithstanding the optimal-tax literature that has developed in recent years, Head argues that equity remains an overriding consideration in tax design, and that the Haig-Simons definition of comprehensive income still provides a practical guide to tax designers. He makes the fundamental point that the tax system serves a quasi-constitutional role in a society. In this sense, the basic rules of operation of the tax system are thus part of the public capital of the community. The attainment of fairness therefore requires those involved in the tax policy–making process to adopt a principled and long-term view, and to focus on social gain rather than personal interest.

The fairness content in the benefit and ability-to-pay principles of taxation are discussed. The paper also notes that even in a system that aims for overall progressivity, there is a place for non-progressive indirect taxes (e.g., sales taxes). This is especially the case if such taxes provide additional revenues to fund government activities that tend to be more redistributive in their impact than most taxes. Head also presents the case for broadly based taxes, except in a few circumscribed instances, such as excise taxes on tobacco, alcohol, and environmental pollution.

Lars Osberg argues for a comprehensive approach when applying notions of fairness to taxation, rather than one that considers taxation in isolation from government actions such as transfer payments and regulation. He also warns against accepting, without further investigation, the conventional wisdom about the inevitable trade-off between equity and efficiency.

Osberg points out the political nature of the concept of fairness, and that any fairness benchmark can therefore change over time, along with prevailing social norms. His paper deals with practical issues in achieving equity, namely, designing the tax-paying unit to achieve horizontal equity; determining the redistributions essential to vertical equity; and taking into account intergenerational equity. Finally, he notes that tax fairness is a matter of process as well as substance.

Leslie Green argues that interstitial equity, despite its prominence in the public-finance literature, does not provide much guidance to a policy maker seeking to design a fair tax system. Such guiding principles are to be found instead in the concept of distributive equity. Three theories of distributive justice are discussed and their implications for taxation explored. These are the libertarian, utilitarian, and egalitarian views. (The last of these approaches is now closely associated with the work of Rawls.) An important conclusion of Green's analysis is that all three viewpoints support progressive (redistributive) taxation.

A. Marguerite Cassin poses a challenge to the conventional discussions of equity in taxation. She argues that the technical language and professional conventions of taxation create a "virtual reality" that is at odds with the reality of ordinary individuals. The (primarily economic) assumptions on which tax statutes and administrative practices are based do not correspond to true relationships among people. Among other effects, the unequal treatment of women in the tax system is perpetuated in this fashion. Cassin concludes that discussions of tax fairness must be preceded by a thoroughgoing investigation of these more basic modes of inequality.

Leo Panitch's paper outlines a fundamental alternative to the neoclassical approach to equity in taxation. Panitch argues that to understand tax structure and changes in tax structure one must deal with the underlying factors in society: the primarily market-oriented, capitalist economies; the distributions of wealth and income in society; and the economic and political power relationships that they reflect. The organization of capitalist economies has set the limits of tax reform exercises, reinforced by the role of the state in supporting private investment decisions, and the dependence of communities and individuals on them. The basic issue on which he focuses is the control of capital. The Fair Tax Commission should see its role, he contends, as educating the public and enhancing the prospects for fundamental structural change.

The papers in this volume clearly and intentionally do not reflect a common position. They therefore reach a variety of conclusions and prescriptions. One can, however, draw from the discussions some common themes. Despite popular cynicism about "fair taxation," these papers demonstrate that it is not an empty concept. Indeed, as a quasi-constitutional structure, fair taxation is essential to the legitimacy of an effective state. Further, in contrast to the emphasis on horizontal equity in much of the recent literature on taxation, these papers refocus attention on redistribution and vertical equity. Finally, differing philosophical perspectives on distributive justice do not preclude agreement on basic principles of fair taxation.

Allan M. Maslove

Fairness in Taxation

Exploring the Principles

1 Tax-Fairness Principles

A Conceptual, Historical, and Practical Review

JOHN G. HEAD

The tax system has long been recognized by political scientists as one of the most important economic and political institutions in a liberal democracy. It has a quasi-constitutional character in the sense that it remains in force, usually with only minor changes, over a sequence of budgetary decision-making periods. The prevailing tax structure establishes the way in which the cost of public services is to be shared and, in combination with the transfer system, has a crucial impact on the shape of the income and wealth distribution. Extremely controversial and potentially divisive issues of justice, fairness, or equity are thus intrinsically of central concern in tax-policy making. Redistributive or zero-sum elements are, accordingly, very much to the fore in public discussion of tax reform issues.

The attitudes and considerations which should be brought to bear in a major tax reform exercise are, however, necessarily of a long-term or quasi-constitutional nature. Single-minded pursuit of short-term political benefits or sectional interest under a system of majority voting will not produce meaningful or durable reform. Primary emphasis needs to be placed on the positive-sum elements or possibilities for mutual gain. A more principled approach is therefore required in which the familiar politics of sectional self-interest must give way to wider considerations that go to the heart of rational budgetary decision making in a democracy. It is, accordingly, no accident that major reviews of the tax structure in modern, democratic societies are infrequent and commonly assign an important role to an expert committee or royal commission that can be expected to take the broader and more principled approach required.

The achievement of a fair tax system in a democracy is rightly regarded as a matter of high economic and social importance. The tax system and the taxpayer attitudes that go with it can properly be viewed as a major item of public capital. If the tax structure is equitable and efficient and enjoys general public acceptance, sensible decision making on public expenditure is promoted. If, by contrast, the tax system flagrantly violates basic principles of equity and efficiency, a collapse of taxpayer compliance and a breakdown of democratic budgetary decision making must be expected.

This study begins with a review of fairness principles, in general, as these apply in the context of institutional design and reform in the modern theory of a liberal democratic state. The more specific principles of tax fairness, notably the benefit principle and the principle of ability to pay, are discussed in a subsequent section, which features a general review of the influential Haig-Simons approach to tax fairness and considers, in detail, some important criticisms of this approach raised in the modern theoretical literature on public choice and optimal taxation. The practical application of tax-fairness principles in some of the more important areas of taxation are then reviewed. This section traces the evolution of tax-fairness principles and paradigms under the impact of changing economic, social, and budgetary conditions and priorities. The study ends with some concluding reflections.

Fairness Principles in General

In view of the prominence of redistributive or zero-sum elements in the tax area, choosing appropriate tax principles might appear to be a formidable task. Certainly, much depends upon a willingness to adopt and consistently apply an appropriately quasi-constitutional perspective. Since justice in the tax area is only one, albeit very important, dimension in the design of a just society or a just polity, a natural starting-point for such an inquiry is to proceed within the broader framework provided by the modern theory of a liberal democratic state.

In the modern contractarian tradition, as reflected in the seminal work of John Rawls (1971) – or in the modern utilitarianism of John Harsanyi (1953; 1955) – an essential feature of a proper approach to institutional design or reform is the application of an appropriately impartial perspective. Impartiality or fairness is achieved in the Rawlsian or Harsanyian framework through the device of a "veil of ignorance" under which participants in the constitutional decision-making process must rely only on general information regarding the nature and operation of society and are denied, or must abstract from, specific information bearing on their own personal or interest-group situation under alternative rules or institutions.

In the absence of specific or personal information on such matters as tastes, values, income, race, gender, and religion, many controversial questions, which must otherwise divide society, may be resolved by unanimous agreement. The characteristically egalitarian presuppositions of liberal democracy, such as equal liberty; equal respect; equality of opportunity; and non-discrimination on the basis of race, religion, gender, sexual preference, and the like, can be firmly grounded in this way. In the controversial area of tax progressivity and income redistribution, it is a remarkable observation, attributable to Paul Samuelson (1963–4), that if all individuals are risk averse – and if, in addition, we could abstract from disincentive effects or efficiency aspects – unanimous agreement could readily be achieved on an absolutely equal division of the national income.

Issues of tax equity or income redistribution, which might appear intractably divisive in the more conventional setting of short-term or annual budgetary decision making, may therefore offer genuine prospects for mutual gain in the more appropriately long-term or quasi-constitutional perspective. For this purpose the assumption that individuals are generally risk averse is sufficient; no problematic assumption of mutual altruism or utility interdependence is required.

It is, however, in the area of economic efficiency that the prospects for mutual gain are nevertheless most obvious and most important. It is also self-evident that, beyond a certain range, issues of equity and efficiency will conflict. In any realistic policy setting we cannot, for example, abstract, in the manner suggested above, from the disastrous consequences for incentives and economic efficiency of an equal division of the national income. More generally, some rule for determining the trade-off between equity and efficiency is required.

In the Rawlsian analysis of justice as fairness, efficiency considerations are rightly accorded high priority. Serious concern about issues of fairness implies a strong interest in matters of economic efficiency. Departures from equality in the distribution of income, for example, could well be sanctioned if economic efficiency is thereby promoted. More specifically, income inequality is acceptable in the Rawlsian framework if, and only if, it promotes the well-being of the least-well-off members of society.

It is, however, characteristic of the Rawlsian system that the standard egalitarian presumptions of liberal democracy, referred to above, are accorded absolute or lexicographic priority. No trade-off of these basic rights and liberties would be allowed. It would, therefore, be correct to say that although efficiency considerations receive their due, equity aspects enjoy a special status and priority in the Rawlsian scheme.

The Rawlsian approach to justice as fairness conflicts to some degree with the generalized utilitarian framework more familiar to tax economists. For a modern industrialized society enjoying a generally comfortable standard of living, the case for the Rawlsian emphasis on equity and on the position of the least fortunate members of society appears, however, to be very strong. Certain types of inequality may be ruled out altogether; and income inequality will be tolerated only if it is mutually beneficial, if not to everybody, then at least to the most-disadvantaged groups.

As against the narrower conceptions familiar to economists, it is, however, particularly important to emphasize that the Rawlsian concept of justice as fairness is, in essence, strictly procedural. Details of the Rawlsian analysis that have been much criticized by economists are arguably less crucial than this procedural emphasis. Such characteristic Rawlsian concepts as primary goods, the lexical priority accorded to an equal distribution of basic rights and opportunities, and the emphasis on the position of the least-advantaged groups are no doubt generally relevant and important. But even these are best viewed as provisional conjectures or hypotheses as to the rules and outcomes that might be agreed upon in the course of an appropriately impartial process of constitutional or quasi-constitutional decision making.

Thus, for example, although the basic Rawlsian concepts and presuppositions may well be appropriate for a society of reasonable affluence, such may not be the case for a backward economy in the early stages of industrial development. At the time of Adam Smith's *Wealth of Nations* ([1776] 1904), for example, some trade-off of basic liberal democratic rights and liberties for increased production could well have been allowed under a proper application of the impartial constitutional perspective. In the matter of income inequality, efficiency considerations might be accorded general priority over equity. The same may be true in low-income developing economies today.

Even if the basic Rawlsian priorities are considered generally appropriate for the modern welfare state as it has evolved in the second half of the 20th century, the institutional details and rules remain to be specifically determined. At this more detailed level, a variety of alternative specific configurations of rules and institutions may all be consistent with a proper application of the constitutional perspective. This point is strongly emphasized by Rawls (1971, 265) in the context of his analysis of budgetary issues, which is much influenced by modern public-finance theory and, in particular, by the concepts and principles set out in Richard Musgrave's multiple theory of budget determination in his treatise *The Theory of Public Finance* (1959, ch. 1). In particular, the relevant general information regarding the nature and operation of specific budgetary rules and institutions will vary from society to society and, with the advance of knowledge in a given society, over time. Excessive dogmatism and exaggerated claims for particular doctrines and paradigms should accordingly be treated with a considerable measure of reserve.

Principles of Fairness in Taxation

It follows that specific principles of fairness in taxation are not ethical absolutes but should be regarded as paradigms or conjectures that may serve, under appropriate circumstances, to shed light on certain aspects of tax design. They are, at best, proximate ideals that may assist the politician, bureaucrat, individual voter, or fair-tax commissioner in the impartial consideration of tax reform issues. It is a familiar observation in institutional design that specific doctrines, which may be appropriate and helpful at a certain stage of economic, budgetary, or social development, may become less relevant as times, priorities, and available information change. This is certainly true in the tax area, and is nicely encapsulated in Richard Bird's important notion of the "tax kaleidoscope" (1970).

Generally, we shall find that taxation issues would be very straightforward if all the relevant facts and information were known. Failing this, it is interesting to discover, as in the case of Rawlsian uncertainty regarding personal information, that ignorance of certain types of general information can be positively helpful in matters of tax design and tax reform. Ignorance, as we shall see, can indeed be bliss, and a little knowledge can be a very dangerous thing.

The analysis of tax-fairness principles in the scholarly literature has a long and reasonably instructive history (Musgrave 1959, chs. 4 and 5). Two broad and sharply contrasting traditions can be distinguished: taxation according to benefit and taxation according to ability to pay. The benefit principle involves the simultaneous consideration of taxation and expenditure, while the ability principle addresses the tax side only.

The Benefit Principle

Under the benefit approach, taxes are viewed in terms of a market analogy as the price of public services. A commutative-justice concept is implied, under which taxes should be related to individual benefits received. In its modern formulation, stemming from the pioneering work of Wicksell (1896), Lindahl (1919), and Musgrave (1959), the benefit approach serves to highlight the efficiency aspects of budgetary policy.

A dominant paradigm here is the "Lindahl solution" in which governments provide pure public goods financed by taxes that reflect individual marginal evaluations of public goods. Wicksell insisted that no individual should pay more for public services than his or her marginal valuation of them or marginal willingness to pay. This may be easier said than done, but the general notion clearly has a resonant echo at the level of individual voters who feel unjustly treated if they do not perceive an adequate return flow of public services for their tax dollars.

In the case of pure or near-pure public goods, however, individual benefit shares are difficult, if not impossible, to determine. At best, tax may be levied on a base such as income, consumption, or wealth, which serves as a crude proxy or indicator of marginal valuation. This problem is obviously especially severe in the classic case of national defence. The problem at subnational levels differs, however, only in degree, as significant "publicness" aspects can readily be discerned, though less easily measured, in other functional spending areas, such as health, education, the environment, and transportation, which figure more prominently in provincial and local spending programs.

The benefit principle nevertheless remains useful – indeed, essential – wherever it can be applied. Many public services have significant "privateness" dimensions and provide specific benefits to identifiable groups, or even to specific individuals. In such cases, a strong emphasis on the "user pay" principle is clearly appropriate, and a more vigorous application of this principle may offer substantial benefits in terms of equity and efficiency.

Although the benefit principle serves to highlight the efficiency or what Musgrave calls the "allocation branch" aspects of budgetary policy – and serves thereby to encapsulate one important dimension of tax justice – the more familiar issues of *distributive justice* are essentially ignored. In the classic modern formulation, the application of the Lindahl solution in the allocation branch presupposes a prior, or ideally simultaneous, "distribution branch" operation to correct any injustice in the existing distribution of wealth or income.

In his path-breaking contribution Wicksell (1896) indeed proposes that *different voting rules* should be applied in the allocation- and distribution-branch operations. In the allocation branch, a voting rule of approximate unanimity would apply, in order to screen out allocatively inefficient projects and to ensure that no individual pays more for a public service than the relevant marginal valuation or marginal willingness to pay. Since the efficiency aspects of budgetary policy relate to issues in which mutual gains are possible, a unanimity requirement appears as the natural counterpart in the democratic political process of voluntary exchange in the market for private goods. The distribution-branch operation is, by contrast, concerned with the more controversial zero-sum aspects. Here, Wicksell suggests that decisions would necessarily have to be reached by majority vote.

Wicksell's interesting proposal for a sharp conceptual and operational separation of distribution- and allocation-branch taxes accords well with modern public-finance theory as represented, for example, by Musgrave's multibranch budget approach. The case for the application of different voting rules as an operational procedure to promote separately the achievement of efficiency or commutative justice in the allocation branch and equity or distributive justice in the distribution branch has not, however, been found generally persuasive. The unanimity rule has been felt by most scholars to be much too restrictive and could obstruct the implementation of allocatively desirable projects. However, Rawls's own version (1971, §43) of Musgrave's multibranch framework provides an intriguing exception.

It is an interesting feature of the benefit-tax literature that particular types of taxes have been regarded as pre-eminently of a "distribution-branch character," notable examples including capital-gains taxes, taxes on speculative real-property transactions, and death and gift taxes. More generally, of course, social insurance systems, with their earmarked and generally flat-rate taxes, constitute the real-world counterpart of the distribution branch of modern public-finance theory. These insights of the earlier benefit-tax theorists are clearly of considerable potential importance in the practical implementation of tax-fairness notions.

The efficiency or commutative-justice aspects of the tax-fairness ideal nevertheless provide the focus of the benefit approach. Issues of distributive justice are, by contrast, the primary focus of tax-fairness analysis in the alternative and contrasting ability-to-pay tradition. It has indeed been argued by Lindahl (1928) in his pioneering contributions to the benefit-tax approach that the sacrifice theories of taxation according to ability to pay may offer practical rules that may be applied in the implementation of the benefit principle, in both the distribution branch and the allocation branch.

The Principle of Ability to Pay

In the ability-to-pay tradition, a tax side–only approach has generally been adopted. The benefits from government spending have been assumed to be largely indivisible. To the extent that this is, in fact, the case, individual benefit shares cannot be determined as required for practical application of the benefit principle. For such common or indivisible benefits, fairness in the allocation of tax burdens would seem to call for the application of some appropriate principle of distributive justice, such as taxation on the basis of ability to pay.

It was in the context of early discussions of the ability-to-pay principle that a sharp distinction began to be drawn between horizontal-equity issues relating to the choice of income, consumption, or wealth as the tax base, and vertical-equity issues relating to the choice of flat or more progressive rate structures. In spite of debates extending over centuries, the results in both dimensions were fiercely contested and largely inconclusive. As Simons (1938, 17) commented, ability to pay is "a basic 'principle' from which, as from a conjurer's hat, anything may be drawn at will."

The Sacrifice Doctrines

With the emergence of modern utilitarianism in the 1870s, greater analytical precision was attempted through the application of the marginal-utility concept. An array of new and competing principles of tax fairness based on notions of sacrifice was proposed to replace or to crystallize the vague and unsatisfactory concept of ability to pay. Especially prominent were the equal-sacrifice principle of J.S. Mill ([1848] 1909), the proportional-sacrifice principle of A.J. Cohen-Stuart (1889), and the minimum-aggregate or equimarginal-sacrifice principle of F.Y. Edgeworth (1897) and A.C. Pigou (1928).

Although distributional aspects were paramount in the analysis of the sacrifice theories, the role of efficiency was increasingly recognized. It is, for example, a remarkable implication of Edgeworth's minimum-aggregate-sacrifice principle that, if we could abstract from efficiency considerations, incomes should as far as possible be equalized, subject to the required revenue constraint, by a process of levelling down the highest incomes. The serious disincentive effects of such extreme progressivity were, however, explicitly noted, and therewith the need for some trade-off of progressivity for efficiency. More generally, the overall burden of taxation to be allocated on the basis of distributive-justice principles was seen to include an "excess burden" or efficiency loss that might also have significant equity implications.

In order to obtain specific results under the sacrifice approaches, a variety of strong and arguably quite unrealistic assumptions had to be made regarding individual marginal-utility-of-income schedules. A choice also had to be made among the various competing principles. Controversial judgements of fact and value were accordingly required, and the results of the sacrifice interpretation of the ability principle were once again fiercely contested and largely inconclusive (Musgrave 1959, ch. 5).

The Haig-Simons Approach

In his classic modern contribution to tax-fairness analysis, Henry Simons (1938, ch. 1) is understandably scathing in his assessment of these early attempts to breathe precision into the abstract concept of ability to pay. Almost nothing of practical value had been gained, over the previous half-century, from the sacrifice doctrines that offered little more than pseudo-scientific window-dressing well calculated to conceal the hidden agenda and underlying value judgements of even their more principled exponents. Meanwhile, the practical challenge of implementing tax-fairness principles in the modern democratic state remained largely ignored.

Simons's influential alternative was to ground a reformulated ability-to-pay approach directly on the underlying distributional value judgements. This is the case for both the vertical and the horizontal dimensions of tax equity. Thus, in relation to vertical equity, Simons (1938, 18–19) argues that the case for progressivity in taxation must be rested on "the ethical or aesthetic judgement that the prevailing distribution of wealth and income reveals a degree (and/or kind) of inequality which is distinctly evil or unlovely." In relation to horizontal equity, he asserts that "the broadest and most objective income concept provides the base for the most nearly equitable levies."

In his original study, Simons has little more to say on the controversial issue of vertical equity. He does recognize that a progressive rate structure may have disincentive effects. He argues, however, that possible disincentive effects on work effort are, in the present state of knowledge, highly uncertain, and represent at most a case for moderation in the design of the progressive rate scale. In the case of saving, he does concede there is a problem, but he argues in a rather modern way that budget surpluses offer a more effective means of offsetting any negative effect on saving. He clearly envisages the need for some trade-off between equity and efficiency, though he would clearly place the primary emphasis on the equity objective.

In the case of horizontal equity, however, Simons goes on to provide a detailed conceptual and practical discussion of the income concept, which has had a truly remarkable influence on practical tax-policy analysis over the subsequent half-century. At the conceptual level, his net-accretions or comprehensive-income concept, defined as consumption plus additions to net wealth, has long become accepted as the ideal or benchmark in the design of an income tax base. Implementation of this guiding principle is, at the same time, explicitly recognized by Simons as posing significant practical problems. The major part of his original analysis, and of a subsequent reconsideration in 1950, is accordingly devoted to the elaboration of practical solutions to major implementation problems that arise in difficult areas such as the taxation of capital gains, corporate profits, imputed rent, in-kind benefits, and gratuitous receipts such as bequests and gifts.

The requirements of tax fairness have accordingly come to be understood, following Simons, in terms of the concepts of horizontal equity and vertical equity, interpreted more specifically as requiring progressive personal direct taxation on a broad income base designed in accordance with the Schanz-Haig-Simons net-accretions concept. It was argued that such a system would also satisfy the requirements of economic efficiency, with the comprehensive income base ensuring substantial tax neutrality among different industries, sectors, and forms of business organization and financing. Disincentive effects on saving or work effort would be minimized by avoiding excessive progressivity in the rate scale. Where trade-offs were required, however, primary emphasis would be placed on the equity objective. On the more controversial fairness issue of vertical equity or tax progressivity, it was generally accepted that the economist qua economist had little to contribute.

Further important contributions to the elaboration of the requirements of tax fairness in the income tax area were made, following the Second World War, by the post-Simons generation of more practical tax scholars, including Musgrave, Vickrey, Pechman, Shoup, and Goode. Significant progress was made during this period on the more detailed practical issues arising in areas such as capital gains, company tax integration, retirement saving concessions, interest deductibility, and the taxation of international income flows. Further dimensions of income tax design were also identified and analysed in detail, notable examples including the need for comprehensive averaging (Vickrey 1947; Goode 1980), the choice of an appropriate tax-unit system (McIntyre and Oldman 1977) and, with the emergence of high rates of inflation in the mid-1970s, the need for inflation adjustment of the tax base and the progressive rate scale (Aaron 1976).

As a result of these and related contributions, the Haig-Simons approach soon began to achieve prominence in major official studies and reports. In this regard, the Royal Commission on Taxation *Report* (1966) in Canada represents a watershed as the first official policy document to embrace and comprehensively apply Haig-Simons principles to the reform of a national taxation system. The Carter Report also had a considerable impact on tax reform studies in overseas countries. Its direct influence is clearly to be seen, for example, in the *Report of the Taxation Review Committee* (1975) in Australia and in the 1982 *First Report: Direct Taxation* of the Irish Commission on Taxation. No fully comparable national policy document was to appear again, however, until the 1984 U.S. Treasury Report to the President, entitled *Tax Reform for Fairness, Simplicity and Economic Growth*, which led to the major income tax reform package embodied in the U.S. Tax Reform Act of 1986.

There can surely be little argument that the more practical orientation of the new tax-fairness analysis, which emerged from the work of Simons and the post-Simons generation of tax scholars, was both timely and appropriate. The central policy insight that important gains in tax fairness, notably in terms of horizontal equity and efficiency, could be achieved without sacrificing vertical equity, by broadening the income tax base in accordance with the net-accretions principle and at the same time scaling down the progressivity of the nominal rate structure, remains of enduring policy relevance and has been widely applied in a number of countries over recent years. The earlier utilitarian analysis as represented by the sacrifice doctrines had, by comparison, manifestly failed to produce meaningful results and had mainly served to divert the attention and energies of leading tax scholars away from the practical challenge of implementing tax-fairness ideals in the modern democratic state.

Changing Priorities and Paradigms

Practical alternatives to the Haig-Simons viewpoint did, however, exist, and received a certain amount of scholarly attention. Particularly notable in this regard was Irving Fisher's pioneering work on the possibility of a progressive personal consumption tax, which appeared during the 1930s at about the same time as Simons's work on personal income taxation (Fisher 1937a; 1937b; 1939; Fisher and Fisher 1942). Like Simons's, Fisher's concerns were pre-eminently practical, though firmly based on strong theoretical underpinnings. Whereas Simons favoured the income concept, Fisher had long been a vigorous advocate of consumption as the most equitable and efficient measure of economic position. He addresses, like Simons, with considerable ingenuity the obvious problems that would have to be surmounted in the practical implementation of his competing tax-fairness paradigm of a progressive personal consumption tax. Like Simons, his primary focus is on issues relating to the tax base, and he has little to say, in the context of his work on the spendings tax, on the more controversial vertical-equity issue of rate progressivity. The Fisher alternative of a progressive spendings tax was, however, categorically rejected on both conceptual and practical grounds by Simons (1938, 94–9, 125–31) and his followers, and, for decades thereafter, it remained at best a minority viewpoint.

With rapid public-expenditure growth and the emergence of the modern welfare state in the aftermath of the Second World War, further changes in priorities and in the conceptualization and implementation of tax-fairness paradigms were, however, virtually inevitable. Whereas the progressive personal direct-tax blueprints of Simons and Fisher had originally been conceived essentially as a single tax system with no significant role for other taxes, the need for a mix of taxes, including company income tax, indirect consumption taxes, social security taxes, and wealth taxes, was increasingly recognized and acknowledged, even by the most enthusiastic supporters of the Haig-Simons approach.

It was, for example, clearly appreciated by most leading tax scholars that the achievement of vertical-equity objectives does not require that all taxes be progressive. A role for flat-rate indirect consumption taxes as an administratively simple method of raising additional revenues required by national or subnational levels of government was accordingly acknowledged. Similarly, it was recognized that the new social insurance systems of the welfare state could quite properly be financed by another flat and broadly based tax in the form of wages or payroll taxes on employees and employers. Rapid public-expenditure growth in areas such as health, education, and welfare clearly signalled a greatly enhanced role for expenditure as an instrument for the pursuit of distributional objectives. Acceptance of flat-rate or even somewhat regressive revenue sources was accordingly greatly facilitated.

Before we examine in more detail some of these broader practical twists and turns of the international tax kaleidoscope, important developments in the theoretical literature need to be considered. Whatever the merits of the more practical Haig-Simons approach to tax-fairness issues – and, as we have suggested, they are very considerable – it would have to be conceded that the emphasis on practical implementation aspects was accompanied by a somewhat reduced concern for theoretical rigour.

The cavalier rejection of the work of Fisher on the merits of the consumption base and the complete abandonment of the utilitarian underpinnings of traditional tax-fairness analysis were increasingly felt by the younger and more mathematically inclined generation of tax economists to have gone too far. The emphasis on equity, and especially on horizontal equity, to the exclusion of the efficiency aspects that had long since become the central focus of modern microeconomics, was also believed to be seriously misplaced. The apparent lack of any modelling of the democratic political process to underpin the value judgements of the Haig-Simons approach was also perceived to cast doubt on prospects for political implementation.

These perceived deficiencies of the Haig-Simons orthodoxy began to be seriously addressed from about 1970 with the rise of the new and highly technical literature on "optimal taxation." The lack of political modelling was also addressed, largely independently, with the emergence from the early 1960s of modern public-choice analysis. Along with developments in the theory of public goods, following the early contributions of Musgrave and Samuelson in the 1950s, there was also a considerable renascence of the benefit approach. As a result, by the late 1970s, it would be fair to say, rightly or wrongly the Haig-Simons orthodoxy had already lost the hearts and minds of most leading tax scholars.

The Public-Choice Critique

Economic models of the political decision-making process typically serve to highlight the dangers, under majority voting, that possibilities for mutual gain, through the provision and tax financing of pure and impurely public goods and services, will fail to be achieved, owing to the malign influence of redistributive or zero-sum aspects. And it is certainly true that the democratic political process can be used to achieve redistributive benefits through the oversupply of public and/or private goods and services of differential benefit to the members of some majority coalition financed by discriminatory or loophole-ridden taxes that fall heavily on minorities (Tullock 1959). A need for constitutional and/or budgetary rules and procedures is accordingly suggested, which would help to limit such redistributive exploitation of minorities and promote the achievement of allocation-branch efficiency and mutual gains.

Among the more obvious implications of these public-choice models would be the introduction of constitutional restrictions on the provision by government of goods or services that are essentially private in character. Alternatively, if such services are to be provided, earmarked benefit-type levies or special assessments designed on the user-pay principle should clearly be required. Other budgetary rules, requirements, and procedures are also relevant in this connection, including cost-benefit and project-evaluation studies, program budgeting, and contracting out.

Apart from the insistence that the user-pay principle be applied whenever and wherever possible, the implications of majority voting models for the tax side of the budget are not in obvious conflict with the Haig-Simons comprehensive-tax approach. It is certainly true that such models serve to highlight the dangers in a democracy that tax concessions and loopholes may be legislated that favour certain industries or special interests. In the rough-and-tumble of annual budgetary decision making in a democracy, it is admittedly not easy to see how the appropriate quasi-constitutional perspective on tax reform and tax-policy making can effectively be preserved. Leading participants approach tax issues from their well-defined positions in the status quo. Equally, however, it seems clear that universality or comprehensiveness in the tax system, if it could be achieved, would help to limit the scope for exploitation by the majority (Buchanan 1976). The real problem, as emphasized in our introductory discussion of fairness principles, is to achieve and preserve the proper quasi-constitutional perspective in practical tax-policy making.

Modern public-goods analysis would appear to suggest, however, much wider possibilities for the application of the benefit principle than had previously been thought possible by supporters of the Haig-Simons approach. In the light of modern theoretical advances, it was argued by Buchanan (1964), Aaron and McGuire (1970), and others that marginal valuations of the "publicness" component of government services at a public level might be determined empirically. Although some progress has indeed been made in attempts to estimate marginal valuations (Bergstrom and Goodman 1973), it could, however, hardly be seriously argued that these estimates could yet provide an adequate foundation for a more general application of the benefit principle in the allocation branch. In so far as marginal evaluations of the mix of public services provided appear to vary mainly with broad indicators of economic position, such as comprehensive income, a broad reconciliation of the modern benefit-tax principle with the Haig-Simons approach to ability to pay may, in any case, be possible along lines already long familiar from the work of Adam Smith. The relevance of capital income in this regard has long been recognized and has been emphasized in recent years by Thompson (1974) and Steuerle (1990).

It has, however, also been suggested, on the basis of the majority-voting models and related public-choice analysis of bureaucratic decision making, that a systematic bias towards overexpansion of government spending must generally be expected under democratic government. This is the general thrust of "Leviathan models" of democratic budgetary processes developed by Brennan and Buchanan (1977; 1980). Observing what they perceive as the uncontrolled growth of government spending over recent decades, Brennan and Buchanan argue that, in the relevant constitutional perspective, the model of a revenue-maximizing government has much to recommend it. Utilizing familiar theorems on revenue-maximizing taxes, Brennan and Buchanan proceed to demonstrate that narrow-based taxes may be preferred on balance to broad-based taxes on the basis of their effects in controlling public-sector size.

This argument clearly goes to the heart of the comprehensive-tax approach and presents a fundamental challenge at the relevant quasi-constitutional level. This objection can, however, be answered in two possible ways. In the first place, it is still far from obvious that any systematic tendency towards overexpansion of government spending can be conclusively inferred, either from the public-choice models or from the facts of public-expenditure growth in democratic states (Musgrave 1981). And even if such a tendency seems a distinct possibility, it still does not follow that the adoption of narrow-based or loophole-ridden taxes represents the most appropriate institutional response. In a more complete analysis, incorporating multiple objectives and multiple instruments, it could well be argued that the setting of explicit tax limits – in the form of, for example, a ratio of government spending to gross product or an upper limit to rates of tax – would provide a more direct and efficient instrument for the control of public-sector size. With possible Leviathan tendencies controlled in this way, the comprehensive-tax base comes back into its own as the appropriate instrument for the achievement of standard tax policy objectives of equity and efficiency (Brennan 1984).

An important feature of the modern benefit-tax tradition, as we have already seen, is the sharp separation of allocation-branch and distribution-branch aspects. The need for such a separation is clearly reinforced by modern public-choice analysis of majority-voting models. Allocation-branch taxes should be designed in accordance with benefit-tax principles in order to promote efficiency and to satisfy the tax-fairness requirements of commutative justice. Pursuit of efficiency and application of the benefit principle in the allocation branch presupposes, however, a prior, or possibly simultaneous, distribution-branch operation to correct any injustice in the existing distribution of wealth or income. On this latter issue, as we have already noted, benefit-tax theorists have had much less to say.

Although it has generally been accepted that a majority-voting rule would be preferable to Wicksellian unanimity for purposes of the allocation-branch operation, Buchanan (1976) has argued strongly for the Wicksellian consensus approach, but applied at the constitutional level, as an attractive solution to the distribution-branch or distributive-justice issue. In their important early contribution to modern public-choice analysis in *The Calculus of Consent*, Buchanan and Tullock (1962) were among the first to recognize the possibilities for agreement on even the most divisive issues of distributive justice under appropriate constitutional or quasi-constitutional procedures in which individuals lack specific or personal information that could bias their decisions on matters of fairness. Buchanan argues persuasively that quite egalitarian proposals on distribution-branch issues might be adopted unanimously and embodied in the fiscal constitution. The often largely separate and independent social security budgets, with their earmarked and flat-rate wages and/or payroll taxes, might clearly be regarded as a familiar application of this general approach in the modern democratic state.

The challenge from the modern public-choice and associated public-goods literature to the long-dominant Haig-Simons tradition in tax-fairness analysis has generally been regarded as significant but hardly decisive. Beyond reinforcing the case, already accepted in most versions of the ability-to-pay doctrine, for applying the user-pay principle wherever possible, the contribution of the modernized benefit principle and associated public-choice analysis to practical issues of tax design and tax reform has generally been perceived as very limited. Apart from a few useful insights on the separation of distribution- and allocation-branch taxes, the literature on political modelling and public goods does not appear, in its present state of development, to offer a generally applicable alternative or substitute for the Haig-Simons approach.

The Optimal-Tax Critique

The challenge from the optimal-tax literature has generally been taken much more seriously by supporters of the more practical Haig-Simons approach. The key role of the net-accretions concept, the emphasis on horizontal equity, the lack of attention to vertical equity and design of the progressive rate structure, the absence of any formal framework for the analysis of equity/efficiency trade-offs, and the informal treatment of crucial feasibility issues have been severely criticized in optimal-tax analysis.

In the optimal-tax literature, the major emphasis in tax-fairness analysis has come to be placed on vertical equity and efficiency. For this purpose the utilitarian framework familiar from the earlier sacrifice doctrine has been refined and extended, and the objective of tax fairness has come to be expressed in the form of a generalized utilitarian social welfare function. A popular functional form commonly employed for this purpose is

$$W = \frac{1}{\alpha}\left(\sum_i U_i^{\alpha}\right)^{\frac{1}{\alpha}}, \alpha < 1$$

where α is a distributional parameter. In this generalized formulation, social welfare depends not only on the total but also on the distribution of individual utilities. The emphasis on vertical equity can therefore be varied, with the Rawlsian emphasis on the well-being of the least-well-off representing a special case of extreme risk aversion in which $\alpha = -\hat{}$. In this more general framework, the trade-off between vertical equity and efficiency can be analysed explicitly, though strong assumptions regarding the value of α must clearly be made in order to generate specific results.

A remarkable feature of the optimal-taxation studies has been the almost complete neglect of the basic Haig-Simons objective of horizontal equity. In order to reduce mathematical complications, optimal-tax analysis has typically been applied in a model characterized by uniformity of individual preferences. Issues of horizontal equity do not therefore arise. Some attempt has, however, been made, notably by Feldstein (1976), to justify this assumption, and the resulting neglect of horizontal-equity issues, in a tax reform setting.

It is not possible here to review in detail the findings of optimal-tax analysis (Stern 1984). Some of the major criticisms that have been levelled at the Haig-Simons net-accretions concept as the guiding principle in the design of the income tax base must, however, be considered. The contribution of optimal-tax analysis to the issue of vertical equity and rate-structure design will also need to be reviewed briefly. In assessing the relevance of the optimal-tax critique of Haig-Simons and the prospects for the development of a practical alternative based on optimal-tax principles, much depends, as we shall see, on the sort of general information available to the decision maker in the application of the appropriately quasi-constitutional procedure under the "veil of ignorance."

The Comprehensive Tax Base

In the utilitarian framework of optimal-tax analysis, the measure of economic position must clearly be redefined in terms of utility. Horizontal equity accordingly requires that, if two individuals have the same utility before tax, they should enjoy the same utility after tax. In two related papers, Musgrave (1976) (from the Haig-Simons school) and Feldstein (1976) (from the optimal-tax approach) have re-examined the net-accretions concept in this more general framework under a variety of assumptions regarding individual preferences and options or abilities. However, difficult conundrums long familiar from an earlier generation of sacrifice analysis then arise. Thus, for example, individual capacities to enjoy income may differ, but clearly cannot be known. In order to avoid discrimination on the basis of taste, the net-accretions concept should ideally include a value for leisure and, even less realistically, allowance should also be made for differences in job satisfaction associated with particular types of work. Where individuals have different types of ability, further problems arise and complicated adjustments would be necessary.

Since all this is hardly possible, it follows that the net-accretions concept can fully satisfy the requirements of horizontal equity only in a model with identical preferences and a single type of ability. It is on the basis of these absurd assumptions that Feldstein (1976, 94–7) purports to demonstrate the total irrelevancy of the Haig-Simons approach to issues of horizontal equity in a tax reform setting. In the equal-preference model, any established tax system, however loophole-ridden, must be horizontally equitable. Base-broadening tax reforms, designed in accordance with the comprehensive income principle, can only result in discrimination among pre-tax equals, though some efficiency benefits may still be claimed. This well-known analysis by Feldstein nicely illustrates his important policy distinction between issues of tax design and tax reform. No such assumption of equal preferences would, however, be accepted by proponents of the Haig-Simons approach; the ideal of the comprehensive tax base remains highly relevant to horizontal-equity issues in the unequal-preference model.

The practical issues posed by leisure, psychic income, and the like must, however, be satisfactorily handled if the net-accretions concept is to be successfully translated into a practicable formula for taxation policy. And this, indeed, has been the central concern of Simons and the post-Simons school of more practical tax scholars. In this regard, the Haig-Simons emphasis on the need for precision and measurability in the basic concepts still seems entirely appropriate. While recognizing that the requirements of equity and objectivity may conflict, Simons argued strongly that subjective considerations of fairness must give way to the demands of objectivity: "the former leads back into the utter darkness of 'ability' and 'faculty.'" Some of the utilitarian conundrums turned up by Musgrave and Feldstein in their respective papers serve only to lend further weight to Simons's warnings. At the conceptual level, the utilitarian approach to issues of horizontal equity and to the definition of a proximate-ideal-income concept contributes little but confusion.

In related empirical work, however, measures of horizontal inequity have been developed, based on the utilitarian notion that taxes should not change the utility ranking of individuals. Since such measures depend on the extent of reranking, rather than on the magnitude of the tax discrimination among pre-tax equals, the fundamental Haig-Simons distinction between horizontal and vertical equity has become blurred and threatens to disappear altogether. Indeed, it has been argued strongly by Kaplow (1989), in an important paper, that this basic distinction is entirely problematic. If vertical inequity is conceived, following Simons, in terms of a degree or kind of inequality that is entirely arbitrary and lacks any moral justification, how can it follow that pre-tax equals should be treated equally? Their equal incomes could well reflect some type of economic injustice, which could, in principle, be corrected by some appropriate degree or kind of horizontal discrimination in the tax system.[1] In a practical tax design or tax reform setting, however, such information is unlikely to be known. If arbitrary discrimination is to be avoided, those with equal pre-tax incomes should therefore be taxed equally, and the distinction between horizontal and vertical equity is restored. Where specific types or sources of injustice can be identified, they should generally be addressed, using other policy instruments, such as labour market and incomes policies.

No doubt, the most fundamental challenge to the Haig-Simons approach in the area of tax base design relates, however, to the informal and technically unsophisticated handling of crucial feasibility and practicability issues. If information and administration were without cost and the policy maker virtually omniscient, the ideal net-accretions concept would be perfectly feasible and could be implemented with appropriate allowance for leisure, household production, psychic income, and the like. When, however, it is recognized that the conceptual ideal of a comprehensive tax base cannot be attained in practice on account of major administrative or political acceptability problems, the Haig-Simons case for pursuing maximum feasible comprehensiveness and uniformity of tax treatment becomes, at best, very unclear. Issues of second-best arise, and the practical policy thrust of the Haig-Simons approach appears blunted, if not completely lost.

The serious implications of the existence of administrative or other constraints for the guiding Haig-Simons principles of tax comprehensiveness and uniformity have been explored by optimal-tax theorists primarily in relation to the efficiency objective. In one of the earliest and most important contributions to optimal-tax analysis, Corlett and Hague (1953–4) have demonstrated that, if leisure is non-taxable, the second-best tax system requires specific departures from comprehensiveness and uniformity involving higher rates of tax on leisure complements and lower rates of tax on leisure substitutes. In a somewhat more general setting, but ignoring cross-substitution effects, Ramsey (1927) had already demonstrated that if one good cannot be taxed, the second-best requires unequal tax rates on the various taxable commodities inversely related to their own price elasticities. These and other examples of cases in which specific departures from uniformity of tax treatment would promote efficiency objectives have been developed and reiterated almost ad nauseam in the optimal-tax literature of the past 20 years.

In stark contrast to the comprehensive-tax approach of the Haig-Simons school, or indeed to the corresponding emphasis in the Fisher-Kaldor expenditure-tax tradition, or in standard public-finance analysis of broadly based, indirect tax systems, the practical ideal which emerges from optimal-tax analysis is clearly one of *selectivity and non-uniformity*. Although largely neglected by optimal-tax theorists, a similar analysis is also possible in the case of the *horizontal-equity objective* and leads to analogous conclusions (Brennan 1972).

There are, however, obvious problems associated with the contrasting paradigm of selectivity and non-uniformity that emerges from the optimal-tax framework. This is easily seen when we consider the informational requirements of these second-best tax systems. In a fairly general model of differing tastes but identical incomes, the Corlett and Hague analysis would clearly require different rates of tax for different consumers of the same product, depending upon the different relationships of complementarity and substitutability between leisure and the various commodities in the preference functions of consumers. Indeed, the point has often been made that, in a fully general analysis, a different rate of tax should ideally be applied to every economic transaction (Institute for Fiscal Studies 1978, 27).

This *reductio ad absurdum* of optimal-tax analysis, though no doubt unfair to many of its more policy-oriented practitioners, serves to highlight the prodigious informational requirements of second-best tax systems. Because of misspecification of the relevant constraints, the second-best tax systems derived in optimal-tax analysis frequently appear just as demanding – informationally, administratively, and politically – as the comprehensive-tax ideal (Head 1982). Although there have been significant advances in econometric estimation, knowledge of the relevant elasticities and cross-elasticities is seldom fully reliable. Moreover, once the quasi-constitutional principle of comprehensiveness and uniformity is surrendered, and in the absence of any really well-defined alternative, the way is open, under democratic political-decision making, for wholesale departures from uniformity based on sectional interest rather than on probabilistic calculations of efficiency or horizontal-equity gains.

In this choice among competing paradigms, much clearly depends upon the extent and reliability of the relevant parameter estimates available to the policy maker. For the first 50 years of the modern income tax system, and certainly during the 1930s, when the income and consumption tax paradigms of Simons and Fisher were first promulgated, preponderant ignorance of the relevant elasticities and cross-elasticities would clearly have to be assumed. In this setting, as Brennan and McGuire (1975) have demonstrated, there is a very strong presumption in favour of comprehensiveness and strict uniformity, since the expected costs of unjustified departures from uniformity must exceed the expected benefits if the departure should happen to be allocatively justified. A similar argument applies in the case of horizontal equity. Of crucial importance here, as in the case of Harberger's well-known analysis, is the existence of a quadratic relationship between the tax rate and the welfare cost, or horizontal-equity measure (Harberger 1964; Brennan 1971).

It appears, therefore, that the guiding principle of uniformity or comprehensiveness in tax base design, which is a common cornerstone of the Haig-Simons approach, the Fisher-Kaldor consumption tax, and the general sales tax, has a fully rigorous justification in the case of preponderant ignorance of the relevant parameter values. A similar justification of the competing paradigms of optimal-tax analysis requires, by contrast, extensive, detailed, and reliable information on the various elasticities. These latter paradigms would seem relevant only in special and carefully circumscribed applications of excise taxation to cases of large uncompensated externalities in such areas as liquor and tobacco consumption or pollution of the environment.

It is interesting to observe that the differences on this issue between the optimal-tax school and the more practically oriented Haig-Simons, Fisher-Kaldor, or broadly based sales tax traditions have narrowed significantly in more recent years. By 1990, it was generally conceded by leading exponents of the optimal-tax approach that problems of information, administration, and political-decision making must rule out any far-reaching application of the selectivity principle in developed democratic societies.

For the period in which it was originally promulgated, the comprehensiveness principle, as we find it in the Haig-Simons income tax framework or in the Fisher-Kaldor consumption tax framework, is therefore entirely appropriate. As long as there remains a significant degree of uncertainty and instability in the elasticity estimates, what we know from modern public-choice analysis regarding the functioning of democratic political processes would seem to suggest that arguments for departures from quasi-constitutional tax-fairness principles of comprehensiveness and uniformity should continue to bear a heavy burden of proof. In this respect at least, it is clearly true that ignorance is indeed bliss and that a little knowledge can be a dangerous thing.

Income Base versus Consumption Base

Information problems are once again at the fore in related attempts, using optimal-tax analysis, to clarify the choice between income and consumption as the comprehensive tax base. Much attention has been devoted, in this regard, to the analysis of life-cycle models in which rational individuals, blessed with perfect foresight and faced with perfect capital markets, plan their consumption and savings decisions with a view to maximizing their lifetime utility. This analysis serves to highlight an important difference between the income base and the consumption base in the intertemporal-choice setting.

On certain further simplifying assumptions, it is easy to show, in this setting, that the burden of the consumption tax is independent of the pattern of lifetime earnings and lifetime consumption. The consumption tax is, accordingly, neutral in its effects on consumption-saving choice and will not discriminate among individuals with the same lifetime incomes but different intertemporal-consumption preferences or earnings profiles. The comprehensive income tax, by contrast, is non-neutral and discriminates against saving in much the same way as a tobacco excise tax discriminates against tobacco consumption. For individuals with the same lifetime incomes, the income tax will therefore discriminate against those with a relative preference for future over present consumption and those whose incomes peak early in the life cycle (such as sports stars).

In a comparison of a fully comprehensive income base and a fully comprehensive consumption base, the consumption base accordingly emerges clearly in the life-cycle model as the superior measure of economic position and constitutes the tax-fairness ideal, from the point of view of both horizontal equity and efficiency. It is, however, a central assumption of optimal-tax analysis that a fully comprehensive tax base is not generally practicable because of information problems and feasibility constraints affecting such items as leisure, household production, and psychic income. Like the Haig-Simons income concept, the consumption-tax ideal is unattainable. A choice between second-best measures is therefore required.

This issue has been analysed in some detail by optimal-tax theorists for the case in which leisure is assumed to be non-taxable, but all other requirements of comprehensiveness and uniformity of tax treatment are assumed to be fully satisfied (Sandmo 1985). In a simple two-period model, it is easy to show that the consumption base remains the proximate ideal if the cross-elasticities with respect to leisure for present and future consumption are identical. If, however, leisure is relatively less substitutable for future consumption, the second-best requires that a higher rate of tax should apply to saving and future consumption than applies to the present consumption alternative. In this case, it becomes possible that income taxation may be superior to consumption taxation from the point of view of both horizontal equity and efficiency.

Since little, if anything, is known empirically about the relevant cross-elasticities, it would appear that nothing can be concluded regarding the choice between income and consumption base, even in this very simple setting. If total ignorance could be assumed, however, in the context of a probabilistic analysis, the case for equal-rate taxes on present and future consumption re-emerges and the consumption base is superior.

Other modifications of the model and of the constraints are, nevertheless, clearly required if a satisfactory analysis is to be achieved. It has, for example, been strongly argued by supporters of the income tax that savings yield a return in the form of security, independence, prestige, influence, and opportunity, over and above any benefits the individual may ultimately derive from future consumption (Simons 1938, 97). In a well-known formulation by Musgrave (1959, ch. 12), the life-cycle model of saving for future consumption is held to be too restrictive. Other possible motives for saving must be allowed for, such as bequests and pure "accumulation." This latter motive encapsulates the "extra benefits" from saving in the form of security, prestige, influence, and so forth; a form of psychic income that should ideally be imputed.

Whereas introduction of a bequest motive makes little difference, on plausible assumptions, to the intertemporal neutrality of the consumption base, the existence of saving for accumulation would imply that *both* taxes are non-neutral and discriminatory. The income tax would discriminate against saving and savers of all types, while the consumption tax would favour saving for accumulation. It does not follow, however, that the income base is therefore necessarily to be preferred.

Advocates of the consumption base, such as the Meade Committee (Institute for Fiscal Studies 1978), who concede the relevance of "extra benefits" as a form of psychic income, have typically argued that some form of wealth tax is ideally required to supplement the basic consumption tax. Although we have little but *a priori* conjecture to guide us, a common argument has been that extra benefits are primarily associated with large accumulations of wealth. Abstracting from leisure-income complications, the proximate ideal would accordingly require a wealth-tax supplement confined to high wealth levels, while the vast majority of taxpayers remain subject to the purest feasible consumption-tax regime.

A case for wealth taxation as an integral, if perhaps relatively minor, component of the tax mix, as a supplement to consumption taxation, accordingly emerges in the context of this attempted application of optimal-tax analysis. Meaningful specification of the ideal wealth-tax supplement remains, however, fraught with informational problems, requiring, as it does, an unknown and possibly unknowable "extra-benefits function" as well as reliable estimates of the relevant savings elasticities and the cross-elasticities with leisure. If, by contrast, preponderant ignorance can be assumed, with reference both to leisure and to "extra benefits," the consumption base can be re-established as the ideal, and both these forms of subjective and non-measurable benefits could simply be ignored.

It is not possible (or even helpful) in such a brief treatment to convey more than a general impression of the many factors that would ideally need to be considered if a completely relevant choice between income base and consumption base is to be made. Even at the theoretical level much remains to be done. The simple life-cycle model, with its unrealistic assumptions of perfect foresight and perfect capital markets, needs to be greatly generalized, and a much broader variety of real-world constraints would have to be acknowledged. Nor is the relevant empirical literature of much assistance. Econometric estimates of crucial elasticities, such as the intertemporal-substitution elasticity, remain fragmentary and highly uncertain (Hall 1988).

The intertemporal-choice issues that are mainly at stake here clearly have profoundly important implications for economic growth and intergenerational equity. Impartial consideration of such matters by decision makers in the present generation cannot, however, be taken for granted. Rawls (1971, §44) has suggested that properly constitutional consideration of these issues requires that the "veil of ignorance" notion be extended, and that decision makers in the "original position" should not know whether they will be members of the present or of some future generation. Regarding "general information," as suggested above, it would appear that, for some time to come, we shall remain for all practical purposes preponderantly ignorant.

The Progressive Rate Structure

Although the more controversial vertical-equity objective of controlling inequality is central to the Haig-Simons conception of tax fairness, detailed issues relating to the design of the rate scale have been almost completely ignored in this approach. In these matters, strong value judgements are clearly required, and it was accepted that the tax economist qua economist has little or nothing to contribute. The issue of rate structure progressivity would simply have to be resolved through the democratic political process. It was, however, assumed that rising marginal rates of tax would certainly be required. It was also assumed that there would be no serious conflict between vertical equity and incentives as long as progressivity was not taken to absurd extremes.

In the optimal-tax literature, considerable efforts have been made to remedy this perceived deficiency of the Haig-Simons analysis. Although the generalized utilitarian framework employed in these studies is itself subject to a number of deficiencies, it has the particular advantage, in the present context, of combining the equity and efficiency objectives in a single criterion or concept of tax fairness. It has, therefore, been possible to focus attention explicitly on the implications for rate structure design of the trade-off between progressivity and incentives. Some of the results obtained sharply conflict, however, with the conventional Haig-Simons position on this issue.

Thus, for example, in his pioneering paper, which sparked much of the more recent interest and analysis, Mirrlees (1971) has examined the effects of the rate structure on work/leisure choice. He finds that the optimal-income-tax rate structure is approximately linear – that is, the structure posits a constant marginal tax rate in combination with an exemption below which negative taxes would apply. The marginal tax rate required is surprisingly low, no more than about 20 per cent, and tends, in fact, to fall rather than rise as income increases. The tax remains quite progressive in terms of average rates, but the rising marginal rates assumed necessary in the Haig-Simons tradition, and so characteristic of modern income tax systems, are notably absent.

The precise results obtained in models of this sort are, however, quite sensitive to the specifics of the social welfare function employed and to the magnitude of key behavioural parameters. Subsequent writers have therefore explored the implications of alternative, and equally plausible, assumptions. Much of this work has involved the relatively simple case of the linear tax on wage income. Progressivity in the tax scale is accordingly limited by assumption to average tax rates. Since transfers, in the form of a negative income tax at the constant marginal rate of the linear tax schedule, are involved, the equity issue is therefore widened to involve determination of the appropriate extent of the entire distribution-branch operation.

Thus, for example, Atkinson (1973) has examined the effects on the optimal linear rate structure of increasing the degree of egalitarianism in a utilitarian social welfare function of the form represented by the equation cited earlier. As might be expected, more progressive tax structures involving considerably higher marginal tax rates can easily be justified in this way. It is interesting to observe, however, that even for the egalitarian extreme, represented by the Rawlsian maxi-min with $\alpha = -\hat{\ }$, the marginal tax rates required are still quite modest by traditional standards, ranging from 30 to 45 per cent.

Much more potent from this point of view, as Stern (1976) has demonstrated, are the assumptions regarding the labour supply elasticity, represented in these models by the elasticity of substitution between goods and leisure. In the extreme case of a zero-substitution elasticity, an Edgeworthian marginal tax rate of 100 per cent, levelling down the highest incomes, would clearly be appropriate. In the Mirrlees study, an elasticity of unity is assumed. The empirical evidence available at the time, however, appeared to suggest an elasticity considerably below unity. Taking what appeared to be the most reasonable assumptions for the key parameters, including a value of 0.4 for the substitution elasticity, Stern derives an optimal linear tax structure involving a marginal rate of 54 per cent and a guaranteed minimum income equal to one-third of average income.

In addition to work on the linear tax, further attention has also been given to the question of whether marginal rates of tax should ideally rise, fall, or remain constant as income rises. These studies strongly reinforce the doubts raised by Mirrlees regarding the case for rising marginal tax rates. Even assuming a Rawlsian degree of egalitarianism in the social welfare function, Phelps (1973) demonstrates that the optimal rate structure in the Mirrlees model could involve marginal tax rates declining from as high as 100 per cent near the bottom to zero per cent at the top of the income scale. The argument for a top rate of zero has also been developed by Sadka (1976), who shows that a similar case can be made for a zero marginal rate at the bottom of the scale. These results reflect the inherent efficiency advantages of a generally declining profile of marginal tax rates; lower marginal rates towards the top of the scale induce additional effort, while higher rates farther down the scale serve to increase non-distorting inframarginal tax payments by middle- and upper-income earners. The magnitude of these efficiency benefits depends, like the optimal linear tax, on the compensated labour supply elasticity. If the elasticity is low, the case for falling marginal rates is much less compelling.

During the 1980s much larger labour-supply-elasticity estimates began to appear, notably in the important work of Hausman (1981), which has served to reinforce these doubts regarding marginal rate progressivity. In Hausman's study of the progressive rate scale applying under the U.S. income tax, efficiency costs or deadweight losses were estimated to amount to 20 per cent or more of income tax revenue. These costs could be reduced by as much as 50 per cent by moving to an equal-revenue linear schedule. Similar results have been obtained by Browning (1987), who argues that a switch to a flat proportional rate structure could reduce efficiency costs by 30 per cent or more. The relevance of such findings for countries such as Canada and Australia with tax-unit systems based on the single individual has, however, been disputed by Apps (1990) and others, who strongly emphasize the higher elasticities that have been found to apply in the case of secondary earners on modest incomes. With leisure and household production non-taxable, a conventional progressive rate structure with rising marginal as well as average rates may therefore promote efficiency as well as equity under a tax on labour income, and no trade-off is required. The theoretical and empirical foundations of the more recent studies have also been seriously questioned (MaCurdy, Green, and Paarsch 1990; Triest 1990).

It would accordingly be premature to suggest that optimal-tax analysis has established even a strong presumption in favour of declining marginal rates of tax, a linear rate scale, or a flat proportional tax. No optimal-tax paradigm has yet emerged that could serve as a really compelling alternative to the specific progressivity presumptions and more general agnosticism of the Haig-Simons approach. Information problems are once again extremely severe. In spite of recent advances in econometric modelling, knowledge of the relevant labour supply elasticities remains highly uncertain. Application of the utilitarian social welfare function also requires strong value judgements, which must ultimately be rendered through the democratic political process.

It is nevertheless a considerable merit of optimal-tax analysis to have brought together the consideration of both equity and efficiency aspects of vertical-equity and distribution-branch issues. The choice of an appropriate tax rate structure is clearly an issue to which tax economists have something useful to contribute, even if some of the more exaggerated claims of optimal-tax analysis in this, as in other areas, must be heavily discounted. The case for flat- or flatter-rate schedules highlighted in the optimal-tax models, although still rather uncertain, clearly deserves to be taken seriously, and the possible practical advantages of such taxes should therefore be carefully examined.

The International Tax Kaleidoscope

In order to satisfactorily complete this conceptual, historical, and practical overview of tax-fairness principles and paradigms, it remains to review briefly some of the more significant practical twists and turns of the international tax kaleidoscope over recent decades and to consider their implications. As we have already noted, the relevance of particular principles and paradigms is bound to change with contemporary economic, social, and budgetary developments. The rise and fall of tax-fairness principles and paradigms inevitably depend on the extent to which they can be perceived as addressing current and expected future economic, social, and budgetary needs and priorities.

The Personal Expenditure Tax

Although the Haig-Simons interpretation of the ability-to-pay approach dominated practical tax policy analysis by public-finance scholars for decades, and the Fisher-Kaldor alternative of a progressive personal consumption tax had been largely neglected, a variety of developments have led over the past 15 years to a strong revival of the Fisher ideal.

Among tax economists, the increasing sophistication of theoretical tax analysis has led to a much wider appreciation of the merits at the conceptual level of the consumption-tax alternative. As we have already seen, the comparison of the two competing paradigms in the now-standard framework of the life-cycle model has served very effectively to highlight – indeed, arguably, to exaggerate – the possible advantages of the consumption tax in terms of intertemporal neutrality and horizontal equity. The practical significance of these possible advantages at the conceptual level depends, however, on the relevant empirical magnitudes. Beginning in the latter half of the 1970s, optimistic estimates and scenarios involving large savings elasticities began to appear, notably in the work of Boskin (1978) and Summers (1981), which suggested the likelihood of substantial benefits in terms of the impact on savings and intertemporal efficiency. Since a progressive rate structure would be applied, these advantages of the consumption tax could be achieved without sacrificing the vertical-equity objective.

Similarly, at the practical level, the possible administrative advantages of the personal consumption tax were becoming more widely appreciated. Building on Fisher's pioneering contributions, doubts expressed regarding the administrative feasibility of such a tax had been much reduced, if not completely eliminated. Indeed, the advantages of Fisher's cash-flow method of calculation in avoiding some of the more notorious complications of the net-accretions ideal in such areas as capital gains, accrued pension rights, depreciation, and inflation adjustment have been increasingly emphasized.

These arguments have been greatly strengthened by the continued failure to achieve anything approaching full implementation of the Haig-Simons income tax in any major country. Many of the most difficult problems are to be found in the capital income area, where, as a result of loopholes, inconsistencies, incentive provisions, and so forth, the allocation of savings and investment has been seriously distorted, with consequent intratemporal-efficiency losses (Jorgenson and Yun 1991). The resulting inequities and lack of effective progressivity have also become increasingly evident and deeply resented. As Andrews (1974) observed for the United States, most modern income tax systems have remained an awkward hybrid of accretion- and consumption-tax elements. Even setting aside the important intertemporal issues, it appeared that standard intratemporal objectives of equity and efficiency could much more easily be achieved through consistent application of the consumption principle.

During this same period, interest in the personal consumption tax moved much closer to the policy level with the publication of important studies by the U.S. Treasury in the 1977 *Blueprints* volume, by the Meade Report for the Institute of Fiscal Studies in 1978, and by Lodin for the Swedish Government Commission on Taxation in 1978. Although perhaps not fully comparable to the Carter Report (1966) in scope and detail, these and related studies had come, by the turn of the 1980s, to constitute a formidable challenge to the Haig-Simons orthodoxy at the practical level. With strong support from theoretical analysis based on the life-cycle model and with encouraging results emerging from empirical studies, the case for the expenditure tax appeared very strong indeed. Among tax economists in industrialized countries, a majority had already come to favour the progressive consumption tax as the preferred solution to the continuing problems of the income tax, though the same could not as yet be said for the policy makers.

During the 1980s, the limitations of the simple life-cycle analysis and of related empirical studies have become increasingly apparent. As we have already noted, claims regarding the theoretical superiority of the consumption tax have now been generally abandoned in favour of a more cautious agnosticism. In the empirical literature, a consensus seems to be emerging, based on much lower estimates of the savings and intertemporal-substitution elasticities, that the benefits of the consumption tax, in terms of increased saving and intertemporal efficiency, would probably be relatively modest (Howrey and Hymans 1980; Starrett 1988; Hall 1988; Ballard 1992). Although, by the end of the 1980s, concern over low levels of private saving had emerged as one of the most important policy issues in a number of industrialized countries, the attractions of the personal consumption tax in this regard have declined significantly.

Among advocates of the Fisher-Kaldor ideal, major emphasis has now come to be placed on the advantages in terms of tax simplification. In part, this change of emphasis reflects the rise to prominence during the 1980s of the alternative wages tax or yield-exemption approach to expenditure taxation, which has been strongly advocated in the work of Hall and Rabushka (1983; 1985), Bradford (1986), McLure (1988), and McLure and Zodrow (1990). As compared with the consumption tax calculated on a cash-flow basis under the Fisher method, the wages tax avoids the need to keep track of all sales and purchases of capital assets. Difficulties in the area of investment income, affecting both the current income tax and the Haig-Simons alternative, are simply resolved by the complete exemption for capital income of all types. The practical advantages of this alternative expenditure-tax paradigm in terms of tax simplification appear, therefore, very striking indeed.

Other aspects of tax fairness impinge, however. Whether there is much to be gained in terms of tax simplification depends very heavily, for example, on the need for supplementary wealth taxation. And this is equally the case for the consumption tax or the wages tax. In the case of the consumption tax, as we have seen, it was argued in the Meade Report (1978) that a wealth-tax supplement would be required to compensate for the "extra benefits" from saving in terms of security, prestige, power, and opportunity. Fisher, Kaldor, and Meade would also insist on the need for an appropriately structured system of wealth-transfer taxes in order to control excessive concentrations of personal wealth. The taxation of bequests and gifts within the framework of the expenditure tax itself, as in the proposals of Kay and King (1978) and Aaron and Galper (1984) for a gifts-inclusive definition of personal consumption, or in the case of the wages tax by McLure and Zodrow (1990), provides further important examples.

With few exceptions, therefore, leading proponents of the expenditure tax would insist upon retaining a significant measure of wealth or wealth-transfer taxation precisely analogous to the problematic dimension of capital income taxation to which they take such exception under the accretion principle. Achieving some appropriate mix of expenditure tax and wealth tax emerges therefore as a major policy complication under the expenditure principle; this is even more obviously the case under the wages tax or yield-exemption approach. As a result, however, the potential advantages of the expenditure-tax strategy in terms of tax simplification would be greatly reduced. Problems of administrative complexity and political disputation, which currently plague the area of capital income taxation, would almost certainly be replaced by comparable difficulties and divisions in the area of wealth taxation.

Issues of interjurisdictional equity and the taxation of interjurisdictional income flows also impinge significantly. Most important, abolition of the corporate income tax supplement to the personal income tax, under a switch to the expenditure-tax principle, would remove a major policy instrument for the taxation of foreign direct investment. Alternative forms of cash-flow business or corporate taxation have, however, been explored that could help strengthen the administration of the personal expenditure tax and, at the same time, serve as a method of taxing direct investment by non-residents (Meade Report 1978, ch. 12). In the case of the personal consumption tax, what the Meade Committee has called the "R + F" base, covering both real and financial transactions, would seem to provide the natural business tax complement. In the case of the wages tax or yield-exemption approach, the "R base" or "Brown Tax," confined to real transactions, as proposed by Hall-Rabushka and McLure-Zodrow, would be required.

As has rightly been emphasized by supporters of the expenditure-tax approach, these cash-flow business taxes offer similar advantages, in terms of neutrality and simplicity, to their personal-tax counterparts. In the interjurisdictional context, however, serious problems arise as the tax is confined to rents, and the normal return to capital is, in effect, exempt. The revenue from foreign direct investment may therefore be much reduced. Even more serious, perhaps, is the further concern, in the international setting, that such cash-flow taxes may not be creditable against domestic tax liability in overseas countries with foreign tax-credit systems.

It is, accordingly, still very far from clear whether there is much to be gained in terms of tax fairness from a switch to the expenditure-tax principle. This is true whether we focus on basic issues of equity and efficiency or on more practical issues of tax simplification and political implementation. Also of considerable importance in this regard is the progress that has been made during the 1980s, most notably in the U.S. tax reform of 1986 but also elsewhere, in the practical implementation of the comprehensive-income-tax principle. If it proves possible, during the 1990s, to sustain and build upon these advances in the implementation of the comprehensive-income principle, it becomes much less likely that we shall see major countries attempting a switch to the expenditure-tax paradigm in the personal direct-tax area. As long as income taxation remains viable and can reasonably satisfy basic tax-policy objectives of equity and efficiency, there remains little incentive to attempt a leap with Fisher into the unknown. The unfamiliarity and apparent complexity of the expenditure-tax paradigm must weigh heavily against its adoption. Transitional complications also present major problems. If, however, it proves impossible to achieve and sustain an acceptable income tax system, this important further twist of the international tax kaleidoscope could yet occur.

Flat-Rate Indirect Taxes on Consumption and Wage Income

Over much of the past half-century, the analysis of the tax-fairness concept by public-finance scholars has been dominated by paradigms of progressive personal direct taxation, whether of the Haig-Simons or Fisher-Kaldor variety. With rapid public-expenditure growth and the emergence of the modern welfare state, the conception of tax fairness defined exclusively in terms of progressive personal direct taxes has been broadened to allow a significant complementary role for flat-rate, broadly based, indirect taxes. Although the Fisher-Kaldor ideal of a progressive expenditure tax has yet to have any real practical impact on the tax systems of advanced countries, the spread of flat-rate, broadly based levies, including sales and payroll-type taxes imposed on the expenditure principle, has been arguably the most important feature of tax structure change over the postwar decades.

These developments have mainly resulted from a greatly changed and arguably more adequate conception of the proper role of government expenditure programs in the pursuit of basic fairness objectives in a liberal democratic society. In this regard, no doubt the heightened degree of uncertainty and personal insecurity generated by the experience of the Second World War and the Great Depression of the 1930s must have contributed greatly to the practical satisfaction of Rawlsian or Harsanyi-style "veil of ignorance" requirements in early postwar budgetary decision making on matters of institutional reform (Dryzek and Goodin 1986). As a result, expenditure programs involving universal free provision of merit goods, such as education and health care, came to be widely accepted as a necessary part of the social infrastructure required for the promotion of important liberal democratic objectives such as categorical equity and equality of opportunity (Head 1988). It was also recognized that problems of income inequality affecting the least-advantaged groups would have to be addressed primarily through the transfer or social security system.

Issues of tax progressivity appeared largely if not entirely irrelevant to these important distributional issues. Since top marginal and average rates of income tax were already high, the substantial additional revenues required to meet these expenditure needs would have had to come anyway from the great mass of the wage-earning population located in the lower-middle to upper-middle income ranges. The incidence of these additional income taxes might therefore be little different from that of a separate flat-rate sales or payroll tax. The higher marginal and average rates of tax required in middle-income ranges would, moreover, add significantly to pressures on the design weaknesses of the progressive income tax and to associated problems of tax avoidance, tax evasion, and political acceptance. Even if the prevailing income taxes could be comprehensively reformed, on either the income or the expenditure principle, similar considerations would still apply. Flat-rate, broadly based, indirect taxes offered, therefore, an attractive and relatively simple alternative method of financing major redistributive government expenditure programs.

The heavy emphasis among public-finance scholars on personal direct-tax paradigms was sharply criticized in the Canadian setting by Richard Bird (1970) in his important "tax kaleidoscope" paper, published during the period of the post-Carter tax-reform debates. At that time, a number of European countries had embarked on major reforms of their sales tax systems, and the worldwide move to value-added taxes of consumption type was already well under way. The possible role of flat-rate, broadly based, indirect consumption taxes as an important instrument for the finance of health, education, and welfare outlays had indeed been highlighted in the North American setting by J.K. Galbraith (1958). By 1960, Sweden had already begun a major tax-mix switch, to be carried out in stages, from income tax to sales tax, and subsequently also to social security payroll taxes (Norr and Hornhammer 1970); a similar switch, albeit in the reverse order, was under way in Norway.

Like Galbraith, Bird argued that the equity concerns reflected in the traditional North American preoccupation with income tax reform could more profitably be directed towards sales tax reform and associated tax-mix issues. A new, broadly based, indirect consumption tax could offer a considerable increase in revenue potential, which could be used to meet growing expenditure needs in areas such as health, education, and welfare. The results of such a change in emphasis could well include a greater measure of redistribution towards the needy than could ever be achieved through reform of the personal income tax, either on the Haig-Simons or on the Fisher-Kaldor principle.

Regarding the appropriate structure of the sales tax, there has long been general agreement among public-finance scholars that the significant advantages in terms of simplicity of this form of tax can be achieved only through strict adherence to standard design principles of comprehensive base and rate uniformity. By appropriate choice of the broad tax base, the sales tax could, in principle, be designed to approximate a flat proportional tax either on personal income or on consumption. Conceived in this way, the broad-based, indirect tax makes, of course, no contribution to vertical equity. Indeed, at the lower end of the scale, significant burdens are imposed on individuals and families who have no ability to pay tax. These burdens can, however, be relieved by other means, such as increased welfare payments or refundable sales tax credits. According to this standard view, the vertical-equity objective cannot sensibly be pursued through the indirect tax system. Primary reliance in this regard must be placed on the personal direct-tax system and, at the bottom of the scale, on the transfer system.

At the implementation level, two competing paradigms of flat-rate indirect taxation have been distinguished, the retail sales tax (RST) and the value-added tax (VAT), corresponding to the two major alternatives of single-stage and multistage administration. Analysis of these two alternatives has focused almost exclusively on the consumption base, in part because of obvious feasibility problems under the retail tax, though a value-added tax of income type would certainly be feasible and has received some attention. In their ideal form, the incidence of RST and VAT, comprehensively applied to all consumption goods and services, is identical and equivalent to a flat-rate tax on personal consumption. While failing to contribute to the vertical-equity objective, the standard tax-policy objectives of horizontal equity and neutrality would be largely satisfied under both RST and VAT, though feasibility constraints would clearly exclude from the base consumption of leisure, psychic income, and the like. Both alternatives have had distinguished advocates, notably John Due for RST and Carl Shoup for VAT.

Until the mid-1970s, the practical differences between these competing paradigms were not considered significant. Over the past 15 years, however, the tax kaleidoscope has clearly turned in favour of the VAT, largely as a result of increased practical experience with that type of tax, especially in Europe, and as a result of more careful economic analysis (Cnossen 1989). Major advantages now perceived for the VAT include the measure of self-enforcement and the clear audit trail under the quarterly invoice system, the more accurate and complete exemption possible in the case of investment goods and intermediate inputs, the more accurate and complete exemption of exports and compensating taxation of imports, and the much broader coverage of services that can be achieved. A well-designed RST still seems, however, the more feasible approach under independent taxation at subnational levels, given the constitutional constraints and vertical-balance considerations applying in most of the older federations.

Practical experience of other approaches to sales taxation over the postwar decades has also served to reinforce the case for strict adherence to standard public-finance principles of base comprehensiveness and rate uniformity. The attempt, under the former purchase tax in the United Kingdom or under the wholesale sales taxes of Australia and New Zealand, to achieve some measure of progressivity through extensive exemptions and rate differentiation is now seen to have clearly failed. The pattern of resource allocation has been arbitrarily distorted, and horizontal equity grossly violated, without any significant amelioration of regressivity. At the same time, the revenue potential of these taxes has been dramatically reduced and the process of their administration greatly complicated. The only important example of a concession that might still be justified is the exemption of food, though even here the case remains far from clear. Indirect consumption taxes, by their nature, are unsuitable instruments for the pursuit of vertical-equity objectives. Income-differentiated consumption patterns by commodity category, if they ever existed at all, have largely disappeared from the scene in industrialized countries.

Nor is there any case in the sales tax area for a general strategy of selectivity and non-uniformity in order to promote greater efficiency, as suggested, for example, by optimal-tax paradigms. Although the relevant elasticity estimates are no doubt more reliable than they used to be, a considerable measure of uncertainty remains. As we have already suggested, once the quasi-constitutional principle of comprehensiveness and rate uniformity is surrendered, and in the absence of a rigorously defined and fully feasible alternative, the way is open, under democratic decision making, for wholesale departures from uniformity based on sectional interest and majoritarian exploitation rather than efficiency. Important issues of administrative complexity are also largely ignored in this approach. Political and administrative experience with value-added tax over the past 25 years has served only to reinforce these concerns. As Henry Aaron (1981) pointed out some years ago in the context of a practical review of VAT experience, maximum feasible comprehensiveness and rate uniformity remain the

proximate ideal in general sales taxation. A compelling case for selectivity can be sustained only in special and carefully circumscribed
applications of excise taxation as a method of charging for major and
highly visible external damage from liquor and tobacco consumption;
for road use, as in the case of petrol tax; or, for the future, in the area
of environmental pollution.

During the 1980s, there has also been another major round of policy
debate, in such countries as Australia, Canada, and New Zealand, on
the appropriate role of broad-based indirect consumption taxes. The
principal issues, concerns, and arguments in the indirect flat-tax area
have, however, undergone kaleidoscopic change since the earlier round
of European and North American reforms and debates. The argument
for broad-based indirect taxes as a means of expanding revenue potential to meet growing expenditure needs is now much less commonly heard, and indeed has come under strong attack both in public
debate and from advocates of Leviathan models of government in
the public-choice literature. While some of these concerns are no
doubt much exaggerated, the tax kaleidoscope has clearly turned,
reflecting the substantial increases in the share of government, slower
economic growth, and increased tax sensitivity among voters, particularly in the major anglophone countries, over the intervening period.

A significant feature of these more recent discussions has been the
attention paid to possible advantages of a sizeable tax-mix switch
from personal income tax to indirect consumption tax within a given
revenue constraint. Such a partial switch from income to consumption
base clearly offers the prospect of some stimulus to saving, though
the likely magnitude of this effect could well be small and would
certainly be less than it would be in moving to a personal expenditure
tax. Useful effects on work incentives have also been claimed, though
such arguments rely heavily on possible tax illusion. A remarkable
feature of recent Australian discussions has been the argument that
tax-mix change can serve in effect as a method of broadening the
income tax base, as income components that escape tax through
avoidance or evasion on the sources side are subject to a compensating
sales tax on the uses side. These and related arguments for tax-mix
change have, however, been largely refuted in more careful scholarly
analyses, by Kesselman (1986) and others. Where tax-mix change
does appear to hold out some prospect of genuine improvement,
comparable benefits could generally be achieved, often more simply,
through reform of the income tax.

Apart from the more obvious exaggerations and analytical confusions, the debates of the 1980s in Australia, Canada, and New Zealand reflect continuing and fundamental differences of opinion between those who regard consumption as the better measure of ability to pay and those who support an income concept. They reflect, in addition, a sharp division of opinion between those who support progressivity in the tax-rate scale and supporters of flat-tax schedules. Indeed, it could be argued, following Carl Shoup (1970), that most of the problems of modern income tax systems can be traced to a misguided attempt to accommodate these widely held but totally irreconcilable views within the framework of the income tax.

Under the hybrid income tax, for example, the income concept still applies across a range of income sources, but the consumption principle is also visible in the concessions for retirement saving, in the treatment of imputed rent, and in an array of investment incentives. The principle of progressivity is likewise still clearly reflected in the nominal rate scale, but major gaps in the tax base typically achieve a considerable measure of effective flattening. The main effect of this attempt to compromise these conflicting principles within the framework of the typical hybrid income tax has been to sabotage the achievement of any recognizable principles of equity and efficiency.

As suggested by Shoup (1970), it is here that tax-mix change might be used to help promote the achievement of comprehensive income tax reform on Haig-Simons principles. In the context of a somewhat broader packaging strategy, it may be possible to gain political acceptance for a more consistent application both of the accretion principle and of a moderate progressivity principle under the personal income tax, by increasing the weight of a broadly based, indirect consumption tax that embodies the countervailing principles of the consumption base and flat rate.

Proposals along these lines involving simultaneous reform of the income tax and sales tax systems were contained in the Australian government's preferred Approach C in the draft white paper of 1985, but they were not implemented. Even more far-reaching proposals were, however, implemented with the introduction of the GST under the Roger Douglas reforms in New Zealand in 1986. Elements of a similar strategy are also clearly evident in the Canadian government's white paper of 1987, which was implemented in separate stages with the income tax reforms of 1988 and the GST in 1991.

The role of flat-rate indirect taxes during the 1990s and into the 21st century will depend very much on likely developments in the structure of the major redistributive government expenditure programs. Demographic trends suggest that the cost of universal programs in such areas as health and social security will continue to grow strongly, and the revenue needs associated with such programs must therefore be expected to escalate farther. A Galbraithian expansion of the role of sales and social security payroll taxes is therefore a distinct possibility.

Public enthusiasm for universal non–means-tested programs on the European model has, however, declined noticeably during the 1980s in most of the major anglophone countries. Tax sensitivity is high, and anti–government-expenditure sentiment is strong. Indeed, the welfare state could fairly be said to have sown the seeds of its own destruction in helping to remove much if not most of the genuine uncertainty and personal insecurity of which any practical Rawlsian "veil of ignorance" must very largely be constructed.

As a result, support appears to be growing for a more selective and perhaps more "cost effective" strategy under which basic liberal democratic concerns for equality of opportunity and for the position of the least advantaged would be satisfied by means-tested programs with benefits confined to the needy. In this way, it is hoped that revenue requirements could be reduced without sacrificing basic liberal democratic principles. If these hopes are realized, no Galbraithian expansion of flat-rate indirect taxes on consumption or wage income need be expected. Debate in the sales tax area could, under this scenario, remain focused on the issue of the appropriate tax mix within a given revenue constraint. It must, however, be doubted whether these objectives are likely to be achieved.

Flat-Rate Personal Direct Taxation

In the Haig-Simons tradition, personal direct taxation in accordance with an accretion concept has always been viewed primarily as a vehicle for the implementation of a progressivity principle, and the same is true for the Fisher-Kaldor alternative of a personal expenditure tax. The rising marginal rates of tax that have been applied in pursuit of this principle greatly complicate the design and operation of the income tax, but there can be little question that the principle of progressivity has enjoyed strong and widespread support throughout most of the 75-year modern history of the income tax in industrial countries. Like everything else, however, views on progressivity and vertical equity are subject to change. In a somewhat ironic further twist of the tax kaleidoscope, the recent surge of support for a flat, or at least considerably flatter, income tax rate schedule offers a serious challenge to the progressivity principle, and indeed casts doubt on the continuing need for a system of personal direct taxation.

To some extent, of course, the progressivity principle has simply become discredited as a result of the manifest failure to make the nominal rate scale even moderately effective. With growing affluence, however, broader sociological factors have also contributed to a noticeable erosion of traditional vertical-equity concerns as these apply at the higher wealth and income levels. Concern with poverty issues remains strong in most countries, but it is, by now, generally understood that these problems must be addressed primarily through the welfare system rather than through the income tax rate scale. Economic objections to the progressive rate scale on grounds of possible disincentive effects have also played a prominent role and have been quite strongly supported by theoretical analysis in the optimal-tax literature and by the results of recent and more sophisticated empirical studies (see "The Progressive Rate Structure," above).

At least equally important, no doubt, have been the serious practical problems experienced in the operation of the progressive-rate income tax over recent decades, and especially since the mid-1970s. These problems are, to be sure, the joint product of complications and failure in the implementation of the comprehensive tax base, greatly enhanced, however, by the need to apply a progressive rate schedule. The contribution of rate-structure progressivity to major and intractable problems of tax arbitrage and to additional design requirements and complexity in the area of averaging and the tax unit has clearly been considerable. If it were not for the desire to implement a progressivity principle under the vertical-equity objective, the complexity of income taxation could be much reduced, though by no means entirely eliminated.

Two competing paradigms of flat-rate income taxation have generally been distinguished: the linear income tax, which is characterized by a constant marginal rate but exhibits average rate progressivity; and the proportional income tax, which has constant average as well as marginal rates. As we have seen, the linear income tax began to receive increasing attention from tax economists in the early 1970s with the rise of the new and more sophisticated literature on optimal taxation. Such attention was, however, powerfully reinforced from the expenditure side by perceived deficiencies of categorical welfare programs and by rapidly growing practical interest in the negative income tax (NIT) as an approach to reform in this area. Although the negative income tax could equally well be combined with rate-structure progressivity in the positive quadrant, the practical advantages of the linear tax schedule in terms of tax simplification began to receive increasing attention.

Among the more obvious practical benefits of the strictly linear rate schedule, the complexities of income averaging otherwise required under rising marginal tax rates to avoid discrimination against those on fluctuating incomes would disappear completely. Problems of income splitting, which are notoriously difficult to control adequately under tax-unit systems based on the single individual, would also be greatly reduced. Tax arbitrage opportunities created by differences in marginal tax rates likewise disappear, though gaps in the tax base could still cause major problems. Integration of corporate and personal income taxes could be dramatically simplified, and comprehensive source withholding would be greatly facilitated. Last, but by no means least, problems of "bracket creep" and the need for rate structure indexation would also be greatly reduced.

The practicalities of the linear income tax in the Canadian setting were carefully examined in an important paper by Kesselman (1982), who concluded that such a system would be quite feasible. Among the various official studies, the linear schedule was also considered in the report of the Australian Commission of Inquiry into Poverty (1975), but was not recommended on the grounds that the 48 per cent rate required would be too high. Application of the single individual tax-unit system in the welfare area, as required for fully satisfactory integration of the two systems through the linear income tax, has generally been considered by most public-finance scholars to be an almost insuperable obstacle. The linear rate schedule need not, of course, be applied in the welfare area, but could be applied exclusively in the positive quadrant. The practical advantages would, as a result, be somewhat reduced, though they would remain considerable. During the 1980s, however, linear income tax proposals of either variety have made little impact on the policy debate.

In terms of traditional vertical-equity concerns, the linear rate schedule preserves a measure of progressivity in terms of average tax rates and provides for the exemption of a basic subsistence level of income. By comparison, the obvious alternative of a completely flat proportional income tax poses problems in a tax-fairness context by imposing tax on those with the lowest incomes. As in the case of flat-rate, broadly based, indirect consumption taxes, however, it could be argued that this problem should be addressed through the transfer system, and specifically through a refundable means-tested income tax credit.

As compared with the refundable sales tax credit, which offers at best only rough compensation based on family expenditure surveys, compensation of low- income earners under the flat-rate income tax could clearly be made precise and accurate. Owing to means testing of the credit, it is true that effective marginal tax rates would be higher over the phase-out range than farther up the income scale. In terms of effective marginal rates, the tax scale would accordingly be regressive. It is claimed, however, that a declining schedule of marginal tax rates accords well with the findings of optimal-tax analysis and could offer useful efficiency gains, though such claims have been disputed (see "The Progressive Rate Structure," above).

The flat proportional tax in its pure form offers, of course, all the important practical advantages of the linear schedule. As compared with a linear schedule confined to the tax system, these advantages are, indeed, somewhat greater. It has also been claimed that considerable effective broadening of the income tax base can be achieved in this way, as the revenue cost of the traditional exemption or tax threshold can be "clawed back" from secondary earners, income splitters, and part-time earners if the credit is means tested on joint income. In the case of secondary earners, however, it is clearly questionable whether equity or efficiency could be promoted in this way. Complexity is increased with the introduction of additional marginal tax rates, and the potential advantages in terms of tax simplification are accordingly reduced.

Interest in proportional income taxation, with its unique threshold-taxing feature, has increased considerably during the 1980s in some of the major anglophone countries. In New Zealand, a scheme for a pure flat-rate tax of 24 per cent was developed under the leadership of the finance minister, Roger Douglas, to take effect in 1988, but was ultimately abandoned in favour of a two-rate system (Stephens 1990, 115–20). A variety of specific proposals for modified flat-rate income taxation with the threshold-taxing feature has been developed by New Right groups in Australia, and a modified scheme was proposed by the federal opposition parties in the 1987 election campaign (Head and Krever 1990). The 33 per cent "bubble" in the modified two-rate structure introduced in the United States under the Tax Reform Act of 1986 reflects the same general approach, though in the context of impressive base broadening.

Although neither the proportional nor the linear flat-rate paradigm seems likely to be implemented in anything approaching its ideal form, the adoption of much flatter rate schedules with, or more frequently without, threshold taxing has been common in OECD countries during the 1980s (Kesselman 1990). In most cases, however, associated base broadening on the Haig-Simons model has been an important feature, and no significant reduction in effective progressivity has been involved. It is not clear from these discretionary reforms that support for effective as against nominal rate-scale progressivity has really much eroded.

Much of the rate flattening, and more specifically the rate compression, that has actually occurred reflects a common failure to index the nominal rate scale. As a result of inflation and associated fiscal drag effects, the range of real incomes over which marginal rate progressivity applies has been automatically narrowed, and a constant marginal tax rate has come to prevail in countries such as Australia, Canada, and New Zealand from income levels little in excess of average earnings. It could perhaps be argued that the resulting degressive pattern of marginal tax rates, with a top rate cutting in at around average income levels, nevertheless accurately reflects broader sociological trends, under increasing affluence, towards reduced social concern about vertical-equity issues at the top of the income scale. It seems much more likely, however, that considerations of political expediency were ultimately decisive, and the vertical-equity issues at stake never received the serious attention they deserved.

There is, accordingly, little reason to suppose that the general slide into modified flat-rate income tax was ever consciously intended or thoroughly thought through at the political level. Although the resulting rate structures offer some of the more practical advantages of standard flat-tax paradigms, problems of excessive progressivity and serious work disincentive effects can arise at low and lower-middle income levels through the combined impact of targeted welfare assistance schemes and the increased compression of the progressive rate scale. At higher income levels, moreover, there still seems much to be said for a modified Haig-Simons view that, while a constant marginal rate may be acceptable over a broad middle-income range, vertical equity nevertheless requires a moderate surcharge or surtax to apply, for example, to the top decile of the income distribution. Failing this, a moderate wealth-tax supplement may need to be considered. Regardless, the design and reform of the progressive income tax rate scale clearly deserves more careful and explicit public consideration in the 1990s than it has received in recent decades.

Interest in flat- or flatter-rate scales has also become a feature of more recent proposals for personal expenditure taxation. A flat-rate personal consumption tax was indeed proposed by Rawls himself (1971, §43) as a suitable method of funding transfers and other outlays. In the recent yield-exemption proposals of Hall-Rabushka (1983; 1985), however, a linear wages tax would be combined with a cash-flow business tax imposed at a rate equal to the constant marginal rate of the wages tax. As compared with the complexities of progressive-rate taxation imposed on a consumption base under the Fisher method, the "simple tax, flat tax" of Hall-Rabushka clearly has important attractions. If such a flat-rate tax on an expenditure base is considered fair and politically acceptable, then it is only a short step to an even simpler system of broad-based indirect consumption taxes in combination with a social dividend payment to offset the burden at low-income levels. The need for personal direct taxation would then have disappeared completely.

It seems evident that this final turn of the tax kaleidoscope still lies much farther down the track. Any feasible scheme of personal expenditure taxation to replace the present income taxes would clearly require some measure of rate-scale progressivity and/or a wealth-tax supplement at high wealth levels. If personal direct taxation were to be abandoned in favour of broad-based indirect taxation of consumption or payroll, the pressure for supplementary wealth taxation would simply be irresistible in most countries. While flat-rate taxation of income or expenditure may well satisfy allocation-branch requirements and fund transfer payments to satisfy distribution-branch objectives at low income levels, vertical equity at the top of the income scale still requires, for the foreseeable future, progressive personal direct taxation of income, consumption, or net wealth.

Personal-Wealth Taxation

For obvious practical reasons, taxes on stocks of personal wealth play a relatively minor role in the tax systems of industrialized Western countries. In principle, a fully comprehensive personal-wealth concept could be defined that would correspond precisely to either of the major flow concepts, whether accretion or consumption, which provide the base for the more familiar personal tax paradigms of the Haig-Simons or the Fisher-Kaldor variety. If it were possible to levy tax on such a broad wealth base, including all the relevant forms of physical, financial, and human capital, the wealth tax could serve as a major policy instrument in its own right for the achievement of traditional tax-fairness objectives of equity and efficiency.

· Such a comprehensive personal-wealth tax is, however, virtually inconceivable, particularly in regard to the human-capital component, on grounds of administrative feasibility and political acceptance. Even ignoring human capital, taxes on a broad personal-wealth base still pose administrative and compliance problems of a high order, notably in regard to asset valuation. Problems of complexity accordingly dictate that wealth taxes be relegated to a supplementary role in tax systems that rely primarily on broadly based direct and indirect taxes on income and consumption.

In the standard literature, personal-wealth taxation has been justified mainly on grounds of horizontal equity, vertical equity, and equality of opportunity. A central argument has been that wealth taxes are required in order to tax the "extra benefits" in terms of prestige, security, influence, and opportunity derived from wealth holding, and especially from large wealth accumulations. Heavier taxation of inherited wealth has generally been favoured, and this appears well justified on grounds of equity, equality of opportunity, and incentive effects.

Among public-finance scholars, it has quite commonly been argued that even the most comprehensive feasible personal direct-tax system, complemented by indirect taxes of the appropriate weight and form, may nevertheless require supplementary wealth taxation if tax-fairness objectives are to be satisfactorily achieved. Actual systems of income and consumption taxation fall well short of any such ideal, and the practical case for supplementary wealth taxes of the appropriate form is accordingly strengthened. The weight and form of wealth-tax supplementation required will obviously depend upon the system of personal direct and indirect taxation with which it is to be combined.

The Role of Personal-Wealth Taxes under Alternative Systems of Income and Consumption Taxation

Where, for example, the personal direct-tax system reasonably approximates the Haig-Simons ideal, there would appear to be little if any need for a broadly based, wealth-tax supplement. It could clearly be argued that the "double taxation" of savings under a comprehensive income tax constitutes sufficient discrimination against saved wealth to account for any "extra benefits" from this source. There is, moreover, significant additional discrimination against inherited wealth since, under the original Haig-Simons income concept, bequests and gifts would be taxed as income to the beneficiary without any deduction to the donor. Over and above the standard "double taxation" of savings, whether for present consumption, bequests, or "pure accumulation" (that is, "extra benefits'), there is a further "treble tax" on savings passing by bequest or gift.

Some leading advocates of comprehensive income taxation, such as the Carter Report (1966), have argued that a supplementary wealth tax confined to high wealth levels could serve as a useful instrument for increasing effective progression in cases where the progressivity of the income tax rate scale is judged to be insufficient but is constrained by possible disincentive effects or for other reasons. Continuation of recent trends towards flatter income tax rate schedules with falling top rates, whether in an attempt to simplify and reform the personal income tax or as the automatic result of failure to index the rate scale, must clearly increase the relevance of this argument. This is, of course, particularly the case if existing hybrid income tax systems are not to be reformed on the comprehensive income principle and where the share of flat-rate indirect consumption taxes is to be further increased.

Where the personal direct tax system is instead to be reformed in accordance with the Fisher-Kaldor ideal of a personal-expenditure tax, the case for supplementary wealth taxation becomes even more compelling, and this point has been acknowledged by most leading advocates of this approach. Even under the purest feasible consumption tax base, the extra (non-pecuniary) benefits from saving and wealth holding are completely ignored. A clear case for supplementary wealth taxation therefore emerges, in relation to tax-fairness objectives of horizontal equity, vertical equity, and neutrality, as an instrument for the taxation of "extra benefits" (see "Income Base versus Consumption Base," above). As an alternative to the separate wealth-tax supplement, some advocates of the consumption base have proposed taxation of bequests and gifts as consumption to the donor within the framework of the personal-expenditure tax (Kay and King 1978; Aaron and Galper 1984). As a method of taxing "extra benefits," this approach has the disadvantage that the amount of additional tax imposed is predetermined by the structure of the progressive consumption tax. Although the degree of "extra taxation" required must involve subjective and arbitrary judgements, the separate-wealth-tax approach clearly offers greater flexibility in the design of an appropriate supplement.

Alternative Forms of Personal-Wealth Taxation

The major distinction to be drawn between methods of imposing a separate personal-wealth tax is that between the annual tax on net wealth and the tax on wealth transfers by bequest or gift.

If it is desired to impose a comprehensive separate tax on wealth transfers, two competing paradigms have been proposed in the literature, corresponding to the traditional administrative alternatives of basing the tax on the estate left at death or basing it on the individual inheritances received by the beneficiaries. Following the former approach, one conceptually satisfactory solution is the integrated estate and gift tax, cumulative on the donor and with a much broadened base, along the lines of the British capital-transfer tax as it applied in the 1970s. A similar but short-lived initiative was the reformed Canadian federal estate and gift tax introduced in 1968. In contrast to conventional unintegrated estate and gift taxes, the capital-transfer tax can be made virtually avoidance-proof, and traditional problems such as the taxation of farm property and small business can be handled by a variety of special provisions. Applied with moderately progressive rates, substantial exemptions, and fully indexed, the capital-transfer tax could well serve as a supplementary wealth tax imposed once every generation.

If, instead, the inheritance-tax principle is preferred, an attractive alternative is the cumulative-accessions tax, based on the lifetime total of gifts and bequests received by beneficiaries. As compared with the capital-transfer tax, the accessions tax seems more compatible with the vertical-equity objective of taxing inherited wealth progressively, and it arguably provides a much stronger incentive for large wealth owners to disperse their fortunes to those with small wealth holdings. A major problem with the accessions tax, however, is that the amount of tax paid is directly related to the frequency with which property is transferred, with resulting incentives to avoidance through trusts and other generation-skipping transfers. As a method of taxing "extra benefits," the accessions tax suffers from the further significant deficiency that the amount of tax levied is unrelated to the length of the period that wealth is held.

It is accordingly of some interest to consider several ingenious variations on the accessions-tax principle developed by the Meade Report (1978, ch. 15), the so-called progressive annual wealth-accessions tax (PAWAT), the linear annual wealth accessions tax (LAWAT), and the age-gap annual wealth-accessions tax (AGAWAT), all of which could overcome these deficiencies. These taxes combine features of the accessions tax and the annual net-wealth tax without involving the need for annual valuations associated with a net-wealth tax. Under these schemes, the amount of tax on wealth transferred would vary directly with the period over which the wealth is held, as it should for the taxation of "extra benefits'; there would be little or no incentive to avoidance by limiting the frequency of wealth transfers as under a conventional accessions tax. The classic proposal for a bequeathing power successions tax by Vickrey (1947, ch. 8) was based on essentially the same general principles. Like any personal-wealth tax, these modified accessions taxes would still pose some difficult administrative problems. These problems could be considerably reduced if rising marginal rates were abandoned, as under the LAWAT. There can be little doubt, however, that any of these proposals could provide the basis for an effective wealth-tax supplement.

Although considerations such as vertical equity, equality of opportunity, and incentive effects suggest a strong case for differentially heavy taxation of inherited wealth, and hence of wealth transfers, there is also some case to be made for the annual net-wealth tax, or AWT (Meade Report 1978, ch. 16). The fundamental argument that the holding of wealth yields non-monetary benefits applies equally to saved and inherited wealth. There may also be some case for extra taxation of all forms of wealth in order to compensate, under either an income or a consumption tax regime, for the failure to impute a value for leisure. The annual wealth tax, striking both inherited and saved wealth at the same rate, may therefore have a role in relation to basic tax-fairness objectives of horizontal equity and neutrality. In relation to vertical equity and equality of opportunity, a progressive-rate AWT offers the further advantage of providing an incentive for the dispersal of large accumulations of saved as well as inherited wealth. As compared with wealth-transfer taxes, the AWT has the additional advantages of reduced discrimination as a result of rate structure changes and an easing of the problems associated with inflation, since indexation of the wealth-tax base would not be required.

The major disadvantage of the AWT, as compared with wealth-transfer taxation, is of course the problem of determining annual valuations for all the various types of assets, some of which have no ready market. In the case of wealth-transfer taxes, valuations are required only when wealth is transferred, such as at death, when assets would normally be valued in any case to ensure a proper distribution of the property. Some of the most difficult items under the AWT would include the value of pension rights and the assets of private businesses and closely held companies. A broad-based annual wealth-tax supplement therefore requires a comprehensive set of guidelines and standardized valuation formulas and could be administered only through a system of self-assessment. The resulting elements of arbitrariness and approximation could well rule out the use of the AWT as the sole or even the principal instrument of wealth taxation. In some appropriate combination with a wealth-transfer tax, however, the AWT might still serve as a useful supplementary instrument.

Recent Trends in Personal-Wealth Taxation

Nowhere in the tax systems of industrialized countries is the gap between aspiration and achievement greater than in the area of personal-wealth taxation. Taxes on wealth transfers, in the traditional form of estate and inheritance taxes, were historically the first progressive taxes to be introduced in many Western democracies, symbolizing the explicit recognition of fundamental tax-fairness principles of vertical equity and equality of opportunity. Respect for these taxes has, however, been considerably weakened over postwar decades by serious structural deficiencies and avoidance problems.

In the case of the estate taxes traditionally imposed in the major anglophone countries, tax burdens on the wealthy were frequently reduced to minimal proportions through exploitation of the concessional treatment of gifts and by the use of artificial trust devices, while, at the same time, increasing burdens were imposed on small estates as a result of inflation and outdated exemption levels. Some efforts at reform were made, but the achievement of satisfactory design standards was rare and generally short-lived, as in the case of the British capital-transfer tax of the 1970s or the integrated estate and gift tax introduced at the federal level in Canada in 1968. The federal estate and gift taxes were integrated in the United States in 1976, but the exemption level was raised dramatically during the 1980s to exclude all but the very largest estates by the end of the decade.

In Australia and Canada, all taxes on wealth transfers have now been abolished. In Canada, the repeal of federal and provincial wealth-transfer taxes was precipitated by the abolition of the federal estate and gift taxes, and the new system of capital-gains taxation was introduced in 1972, with its characteristic Simons-Carter feature of the deemed realization at death and on gift. In Australia, the roles were reversed, with political competition at the state level serving as the immediate cause in the mid-1970s and the federal government joining the resulting bandwagon towards the end of the decade, despite the recommendations of the Taxation Review Committee in 1975. Although these taxes still survive in the United States and the United Kingdom, they were much eroded under the Reagan and Thatcher governments during the 1980s, and a similar pattern has been followed in New Zealand.

Apart from the corrosive effects of the serious design deficiencies and the special subnational issues applying in Australia and Canada, the decline of wealth-transfer taxation no doubt also reflects reduced concern about vertical-equity issues at high income and wealth levels. Here again, the major redistributive public-expenditure programs of the welfare state in such areas as education and income support are widely seen as promoting vertical equity and equality of opportunity much more effectively by directly addressing the needs of the socially disadvantaged. Only personal direct taxes, however, whether imposed on wealth or income, can satisfy vertical-equity requirements at the top of the scale and address the threat to political equality represented by large concentrations of family wealth and influence.

Nor does postwar experience in the area of annual wealth taxation suggest that these traditional tax-fairness concerns could be more adequately met by switching to an AWT approach. The annual wealth taxes of the various European countries are mostly of venerable antiquity and apply alongside traditional inheritance-tax systems essentially as a very minor supplement to the income tax. The newer wealth taxes introduced in Spain in 1977 and France in 1982 do not depart from this traditional pattern.

Particularly alarming in this regard, however, is the case of the Irish Republic, where a new wealth tax was introduced in 1975 but subsequently abolished in 1978 (Sandford and Morissey 1985). The same pattern has since been repeated in France, where the new wealth tax introduced in 1982 was repealed in 1987. Effective introduction of wealth taxation in whatever form clearly requires a basic consensus or political understanding cutting across political parties and interest groups if it is to be successful. In the absence of a properly quasi-constitutional approach, there is clearly a real danger under majoritarian democracy of costly and disruptive policy reversals that simply increase inequity rather than reduce it.

Although, as we have argued above, wealth taxation, if properly designed, can make a useful contribution to tax-fairness objectives, it is also extremely important to "hose down" totally unrealistic expectations. Under modern capitalism, the threat to political equality and the democratic ideal posed by large family fortunes is in most countries much less than that posed by the broader issue of corporate wealth and influence. Nor can this latter issue be addressed in any sensible or meaningful way by extending the wealth-tax base to cover corporate assets. Other policy instruments, such as limits on political advertising on television, limitations on election spending, public funding of elections, public disclosure of campaign contributions, must generally be relied upon.

Concluding Reflections

Majoritarian democracy, if it is to function efficiently, clearly requires much more than the mere pursuit of sectional or individual self-interest and the holding of periodic parliamentary elections. A clear distinction must first be drawn, at all the relevant policy-making levels, between issues that require no more than routine annual budgetary consideration and issues of institutional reform that require a broader approach.

It is a fundamental contention of this paper that tax fairness can be achieved only if there is a willingness on the part of those with some significant involvement in the tax policy–making process to adopt and consistently apply an appropriately impartial and quasi-constitutional perspective. Only in this way can the inherent divisiveness of decision making in the tax area be reduced to manageable proportions, and the potential gains in terms of equity, efficiency, and simplicity from the implementation of a fair-tax system be reliably achieved.

No doubt these requirements are very demanding and may not easily be met. Leading participants in the tax debate naturally approach issues of tax reform from their well-defined positions in the status quo, and there is an almost irresistible temptation to pursue individual or sectional self-interest in preference to the abstract claims of tax fairness.

The broader and more principled approach can more confidently be expected in the case of an independent tax reform committee or commission. Even in this more promising context, however, problems arise, as sensible recommendations may not be found politically persuasive and can be ignored by government. Even if implemented, there can be little benefit from even the most sensible reform measures if they are likely to be soon reversed under a change of government. Agreement among impartial tax-policy makers on a government commission is only one important part of a much wider consensus that must somehow be established, cutting across the major interest groups and political parties, if meaningful and durable tax reform is to be achieved.

If the requirements of impartiality can pose problems, so also does the "general information" that should guide the policy maker in choosing among the various alternative tax systems. Strategic parameter values, such as savings and labour supply elasticities, remain largely unknown. On these and other important matters some information exists, but it is highly uncertain. Problems of tax-policy making would be greatly simplified if we knew much more or if we knew much less. Given what we know about the functioning of real-world political processes, there still seems much to be said for basing tax policy on the assumption of preponderant ignorance.

Given the relevant "general information," suitably processed and presented, the impartial decision maker may still face considerable difficulties. It is, for example, quite doubtful, given what we currently know, whether a clear preference could be established between the major personal direct-tax paradigms of the Haig-Simons and Fisher-Kaldor variety. Within broad limits, the choice between flatter and more progressive rate schedules also remains unclear. Since the major policy alternatives may vary in terms of risk, even the most impartial decision makers may choose differently, and the prospects for agreement can be much reduced.

These problems would exist even if there were no established tax system and we were simply choosing among alternative tax ideals in a *de novo* tax-design setting. In the presence of an established tax system, however, the issue is one of tax reform rather than of tax design (Feldstein 1976). This renders the problem at once easier and more difficult.

On the one hand, the prevailing tax system may be so unfair and inefficient that any of the competing tax paradigms or proximate ideals may represent a clear-cut and very substantial improvement, as compared with the status quo. On the other hand, serious transitional problems can arise in changing to a new tax system. Potential gains may be greatly reduced when proper account is taken of the modifications and transitional provisions required to compensate losers, ameliorate windfalls, and more generally buy off the opposition in order to achieve political acceptance. From a promising initial prospect, the final result can be a reform package offering small and uncertain long-term benefits. It is little wonder, then, that leading participants in the tax-reform process may often rationally prefer to pursue selfish strategies, offering clear-cut, short-term redistributive benefits to themselves, rather than the more abstract and uncertain benefits of tax fairness.

In general, however, the claims of tax fairness and of a properly impartial approach to institutional reform in a liberal democracy remain compelling. It is only in this way that the modern democratic state can be guaranteed to deliver substantial net gains to its citizens and to outperform on a consistent basis any arbitrarily chosen totalitarian regime.

Note

The first draft of this paper was prepared for the Ontario Fair Tax Commission and completed in February 1992.

1 Musgrave (1990), in a response to Kaplow, reasserts the need for a clear distinction, but he does not come to grips with this conceptual difficulty emphasized by Kaplow.

Bibliography

Aaron, H.J., ed. 1976. *Inflation and the Income Tax*. Washington, DC: Brookings Institution

– ed. 1981. *The Value-Added Tax: Lessons from Europe*. Washington, DC: Brookings Institution

Aaron, H.J., and H. Galper. 1984. "A Tax on Consumption, Bequests and Gifts and Other Strategies for Reform." In *Options for Tax Reform*, ed. J.A. Pechman, 106–46. Washington, DC: Brookings Institution

Aaron, H.J., and M. McGuire. 1970. "Public Goods and Income Distribution." *Econometrica*, 38: 907–20

Andrews, W.D. 1974. "A Consumption-Type or Cash Flow Personal Income Tax." *Harvard Law Review*, 87: 1113–88

Apps, P.A. 1990. "Tax Transfer Options: A Critique of Joint Income and

Flat Rate Proposals." In *Flattening the Tax Rate Scale,* ed. J.G. Head and
R. Krever, 211–35. Melbourne: Longman Professional

Atkinson, A.B. 1973. "How Progressive Should Income Tax Be?" In *Essays
in Modern Economics,* ed. M. Parkin and A.R. Nobay, 90–109. London:
Longmans

Auerbach, A.J., L.J. Kotlikoff, and J. Skinner. 1983. "The Efficiency Gains
from Dynamic Tax Reform." *International Economic Review,* 24: 81–100

Australia. Taxation Review Committee. 1975. *Full Report,* 31 January. Canberra: Australian Government Publishing Service

Australian Commission of Inquiry into Poverty. 1975. *Poverty in Australia*
(Henderson Report). Canberra: Australian Government Publishing Service

Ballard, C.L. 1992. "Taxation and Saving." In *Taxation Issues of the 1990s,*
ed. J.G. Head. Sydney: Australian Tax Research Foundation (forthcoming)

Bergstrom, T.C., and R.P. Goodman. 1973. "Private Demands for Public
Goods." *American Economic Review,* 53: 280–96

Bird, R.M. 1970. "The Tax Kaleidoscope: Perspectives on Tax Reform in
Canada." *Canadian Tax Journal,* 18: 444–73

Boskin, M.J. 1978. "Taxation, Saving, and the Rate of Interest." *Journal of
Political Economy,* 86 (part 2): s3–s27

Bovenberg, E.L. 1989. "Tax Policy and National Saving in the United
States: A Survey." *National Tax Journal,* 42: 123–38

Bradford, D.F. 1986. *Untangling the Income Tax.* Cambridge, MA: Harvard
University Press

Brennan, G. 1971. "Horizontal Equity: An Extension of an Extension."
Public Finance, 26: 437–56

– 1972. "Second Best Aspects of Horizontal Equity Questions." *Public Finance,* 27: 282–91

– 1984. "Tax Reform and Tax Limits: Political Process in Public Finance."
Australian Tax Forum, 1: 83–95

Brennan, G., and J.M. Buchanan. 1977. "Towards a Tax Constitution for
Leviathan." *Journal of Public Economics,* 8: 255–73

– 1980. *The Power to Tax.* Cambridge: Cambridge University Press

Brennan, G., and T. McGuire. 1975. "Optimal Policy Choice under Uncertainty." *Journal of Public Economics,* 4: 205–9

Browning, E.K. 1987. "On the Marginal Welfare Cost of Taxation." *American Economic Review,* 77: 11–23

Buchanan, J.M. 1964. "Fiscal Institutions and Efficiency in Collective Out-
lay." *American Economic Review,* 54: 227–35

– 1976. "Taxation in Fiscal Exchange." *Journal of Public Economics*, 6: 17–29

Buchanan, J.M., and G. Tullock. 1962. *The Calculus of Consent*. Ann Arbor: University of Michigan Press

Canada. Royal Commission on Taxation. 1966. *Report* (Carter Report). Vol. 1. Ottawa: Queen's Printer

Carter Report. *See* Canada, Royal Commission on Taxation

Cnossen, S. 1989. "The Technical Superiority of VAT over RST." In *Australian Tax Reform in Retrospect and Prospect*, ed. J.G. Head, 325–59. Sydney: Australian Tax Research Foundation

Cohen-Stuart, A.J. 1889. *Bijdrage tot de Theorie der progressieve Inkomstenbelasting*. The Hague: Martinus Nijhoff

Commonwealth of Australia. 1985. *Reform of the Australian Tax System*. Draft White Paper. Canberra: Australian Government Publishing Service

Corlett, W.J., and D.C. Hague. 1953–4. "Complementarity and the Excess Burden of Taxation." *Review of Economic Studies*, 21: 21–30

Dryzek, J., and R.E. Goodin. 1986. "Risk-Sharing and Social Justice: The Motivational Foundations of the Postwar Welfare State." *British Journal of Political Science*, 16: 1–34

Edgeworth, F.Y. 1897. "The Pure Theory of Taxation." *Economic Journal*, 7: 100–22

Feldstein, M. 1976. "On the Theory of Tax Reform." *Journal of Public Economics*, 6: 77–104

Fisher, I. 1937a. "A Practical Schedule for an Income Tax." *The Tax Magazine*, July, 1–13

– 1937b. "Income in Theory and Income Taxation in Practice." *Econometrica*, 5: 1–55

– 1939. "Double Taxation of Savings." *American Economic Review*, 29: 16–33

Fisher, I., and H.W. Fisher. 1942. *Constructive Income Taxation*. New York: Harper Bros.

Galbraith, J.K. 1958. *The Affluent Society*. Boston: Houghton Mifflin

Goode, R. 1980. "Long-Term Averaging of Income for Tax Purposes." In *The Economics of Taxation*, ed. H.J. Aaron and M.J. Boskin, 159–78. Washington, DC: Brookings Institution

– 1991. "Changing Views of the Personal Income Tax." In *Retrospectives on Public Finance*, ed. L. Eden, 93–117. Durham, NC: Duke University Press

Hall, R.E. 1988. "Intertemporal Substitution in Consumption." *Journal of Political Economy*, 96: 339–57

Hall, R.E., and A. Rabushka. 1983. *Low Tax, Simple Tax, Flat Tax.* New York: McGraw-Hill

– 1985. *The Flat Tax.* Stamford, CT: Hoover Institution

Harberger, A.C. 1964. "Taxation, Resource Allocation and Welfare." In *The Role of Direct and Indirect Taxes in the Federal Revenue System.* A Conference Report of the National Bureau of Economic Research and the Brookings Institution, 25–80. Princeton, NJ: Princeton University Press

Harsanyi, J.C. 1953. "Cardinal Utility in Welfare Economics and in the Theory of Risk-Taking." *Journal of Political Economy,* 61: 434–5

– 1955. "Cardinal Welfare, Individualistic Ethics and Interpersonal Comparisons of Utility" *Journal of Political Economy,* 63: 309–21

Hausman, J.A. 1981. "Labor Supply." In *How Taxes Affect Economic Behaviour,* ed. H.J. Aaron and J. Pechman, 27–72. Washington, DC: Brookings Institution

Head, J.G. 1979. "The Simons-Carter Approach to Tax Policy: A Reappraisal." In *Wirtschaftswissenschaft als Grundlage staatlichen Handelns,* ed. P. Bohley and G. Tolkemitt, 191–222. Tübingen: J.C.B. Mohr (Paul Siebeck)

– 1982. "The Comprehensive Tax Base Revisited." *Finanzarchiv,* 40: 193–210

– 1988. "On Merit Wants." *Finanzarchiv,* 46: 1–37

Head, J.G., and R. Krever, eds. 1990. *Flattening the Tax Rate Scale.* Melbourne: Longmans

Howrey, E.P., and S.J. Hymans. 1980. "The Measurement and Determination of Loanable Funds Saving." In *What Should Be Taxed: Income or Expenditure?* ed. J. Pechman, 1–48. Washington, DC: Brookings Institution

Institute for Fiscal Studies. 1978. *The Structure and Reform of Direct Taxation: Report of a Committee Chaired by Prof. J.E. Meade* (Meade Report). London: Allen and Unwin

Irish Commission on Taxation. 1982. *First Report: Direct Taxation.* Dublin: Stationery Office

Jorgenson, D.W., and K.Y Yun. 1991. *Tax Reform and the Cost of Capital.* Oxford: Clarendon Press

Kaldor, N. 1955. *An Expenditure Tax.* London: Allen and Unwin

Kaplow, L. 1989. "Horizontal Equity: Measures in Search of a Principle." *National Tax Journal,* 42: 139–54

Kay, J.A., and M.A. King. 1978. *The British Tax System.* Oxford: Oxford University Press

Kesselman, J. 1982. "Taxpayer Behavior and the Design of a Credit Income Tax." In *Income-Tested Transfer Programs: The Case For and Against,* ed. I. Garfinkel, 215–90. New York: Academic Press

- 1986. "The Role of the Tax Mix in Tax Reform." In *Changing the Tax Mix*, ed. J.G. Head, 1–51. Sydney: Australian Tax Research Foundation
- 1990. *Rate Structure and Personal Taxation: Flat Rate or Dual Rate?* Wellington, NZ: Victoria University Press

Lindahl, E. 1919. *Die Gerechtigkeit der Besteuerung.* Lund: Gleerupsa
- 1928. "Einige strittige Fragen der Steuertheorie." In *Die Wirtschaftstheorie der Gegenwart*, ed. H. Mayer, 282–304. Vienna: Springer-Verlag

Lodin, S. 1978. *Progressive Expenditure Tax – An Alternative? A Report of the 1972 Government Commission on Taxation.* Stockholm: LiberForlag

MaCurdy, T., D. Green, and H. Paarsch. 1990. "Assessing Empirical Approaches for Analysing Taxes and Labor Supply." *Journal of Human Resources*, 25: 415–90

McIntyre, M.J., and O. Oldman. 1977. "Taxation of the Family in a Comprehensive and Simplified Income Tax." *Harvard Law Review*, 90: 1573–1630

McLure, Jr, C.E., 1988. "The 1986 Tax Act. Tax Reform's Finest Hour or Death Throes of the Income Tax?" *National Tax Journal*, 41: 303–15

McLure, Jr, C.E., and G.R. Zodrow. 1990. "Administrative Aspects of a Consumption-based Tax System." In *Heidelberg Congress on Taxing Consumption*, ed. M. Rose, 335–89. Berlin and New York: Springer-Verlag

Meade Report. *See* Institute for Fiscal Studies

Mill, J.S. [1848] 1909. *Principles of Political Economy*, ed. W.J. Ashley. London: Longmans

Mirrlees, J.A. 1971. "An Exploration in the Theory of Optimal Income Taxation." *Review of Economic Studies*, 38: 179–208

Mueller, D.C. 1989. *Public Choice II.* Cambridge: Cambridge University Press

Musgrave, R.A. 1959. *The Theory of Public Finance.* New York: McGraw-Hill
- 1976. "ET, OT and SBT." *Journal of Public Economics*, 6: 3–16
- 1981. "Leviathan Cometh – Or Does He?" In *Tax and Expenditure Limitations*, ed. H. Ladd and T.N. Tideman, 77–120. Washington, DC: Urban Institute Press
- 1990. "Horizontal Equity, Once More." *National Tax Journal*, 43: 113–22

Norr, M., and N.G. Hornhammer. 1970. "The Value-Added Tax in Sweden." *Columbia Law Review*, 70: 379–422

Phelps, E.S. 1973. "Taxation of Wage Income for Economic Justice." *Quarterly Journal of Economics*, 87: 331–54

Pigou, A.C. 1928. *A Study in Public Finance.* London: Macmillan

Ramsey, F.P. 1927. "A Contribution to the Theory of Taxation." *Economic Journal*, 37: 47–61

Rawls, J. 1971. *A Theory of Justice.* Cambridge, MA: Harvard University Press

Sadka, E. 1976. "On Income Distribution, Incentive Effects and Optimal Income Taxation." *Review of Economic Studies,* 43: 261–7

Samuelson, P.A. 1963–4. "A.P. Lerner at Sixty." *Review of Economic Studies,* 31: 169–78

Sandford, C.T., and O. Morissey. 1985. *The Irish Wealth Tax – A Case Study in Economics and Politics.* Dublin: Economic and Social Research Institute

Sandmo, A. 1985. "The Effects of Taxation on Savings and Risk Taking." In Handbook of Public Economics, vol. 1., ed. A.J. Auerbach and M. Feldstein, 265–311. New York: North-Holland

Shoup, C.S. 1970. "Tax Reform." In *Theorie und Praxis des finanzpolitischen Interventionismus,* ed. H. Haller, Lore Kullmer, and Herbert-Timm, 245–52. Tübingen: J.C.B. Mohr (Paul Siebeck)

Simons, H.C. 1938. *Personal Income Taxation.* Chicago: University of Chicago Press

– 1950. *Federal Tax Reform.* Chicago: University of Chicago Press

Smith, A. [1776] 1904. *The Wealth of Nations,* ed. E. Cannan. New York: Putnam

Starrett, D.A. 1988. "Effects of Taxes on Saving." In *Uneasy Compromise: Problems of a Hybrid Income-Consumption Tax,* ed. H.J. Aaron, H. Galper, and J.A. Pechman, 237–68. Washington, DC: Brookings Institution

Stephens, R.J. 1990. "Flattening the Tax Rate Scale in New Zealand." In *Flattening the Tax Rate Scale,* ed. J.G. Head and R. Krever, 103–37. Melbourne: Longmans

Stern, N.H. 1976. "On the Specification of Models of Optimum Income Taxation." *Economics and Politics,* 6: 123–62

– 1984. "Optimum Taxation and Tax Policy." *IMF STAFF PAPERS,* 31: 339–78

– 1990. "Uniformity versus Selectivity in Indirect Taxation." *Economics and Politics,* 2 (1): 82–108

Steuerle, E. 1990. "Capital Income and the Future of the Income Tax." In *The Personal Income Tax: Phoenix from the Ashes?* ed. S. Cnossen and R.M. Bird, 211–27. New York: North-Holland

Summers, L.H. 1981. "Capital Taxation and Accumulation in a Life-Cycle Growth Model." *American Economic Review,* 71: 533–44

Tait, A. 1989. "Not So General Equilibrium and Not So Optimal Taxation." *Public Finance,* 44: 169–82

Thompson, E.A. 1974. "Taxation and National Defence." *Journal of Political Economy,* 82: 755–82

Triest, R.K. 1990. "The Effect of Income Taxation on Labor Supply in the United States." *Journal of Human Resources*, 25: 491–516

Tullock, G. 1959. "Some Problems of Majority Voting." *Journal of Political Economy*, 67: 571–9

United States. Department of the Treasury. 1977. *Blueprints for Basic Tax Reform*. Washington, DC: Government Printing Office

– 1984. *Tax Reform for Fairness, Simplicity and Economic Growth*. Washington, DC: Government Printing Office

Vickrey, W. 1947. *Agenda for Progressive Taxation*. New York: Ronald Press

Wicksell, K. 1896. *Finanztheoretische Untersuchungen*. Jena: Fischer

2 What's Fair?

The Problem of Equity in Taxation

LARS OSBERG

Equity in taxation is important for both principled and practical reasons. Citizens have, in general, the right to expect "fairness" in public policy, including taxation. As well, since tax systems perceived to be "unfair" tend to be resisted with special intensity, such tax systems tend to generate less revenue, and have higher administrative costs, than tax systems that are perceived to be "fair." However, it is not immediately obvious what a "fair" tax system would look like. Section 1 of this paper, therefore, begins with four real-world tax examples rationalized by differing concepts of "equity." Section 2 then discusses what is meant by taxation and the realism of considering fairness in taxation in isolation from transfer payments, regulation, and other government activities. Section 3 cautions readers against premature presumptions of "trade-offs."

Since society is continually changing, the passage of time affects the concept of equity in taxation, as well as its practical implementation, as section 4 discusses. Section 5 then considers how one might define the tax-paying unit and the measure of tax-paying capacity so that the ideal of "horizontal equity" – that "similar" taxpayers should be treated in a "similar" fashion – could be satisfied. Section 6 examines the issue of user fees, then section 7 turns to the idea that "vertical" equity implies that taxpayers with greater ability to pay should pay more tax. Section 8 argues that if one wants to maintain equity between generations, one cannot ignore the impact of taxation on growth, capital formation, and the natural and social environment. Section 9 notes that the criterion of "fairness" must be applied both to the process by which income is distributed and to the outcomes of that process – "equality of opportunity" is an important dimension of fairness. Section 10 offers concluding remarks.

1 Examples of Equity

The following four examples illustrate different dimensions of the concept of equity:

- The driver's licence renewal fee is the same for all motorists, and of course is zero for all non-drivers. It would be considered unfair to charge some drivers more than others for licence renewal – the principle of "horizontal equity" requires that individuals who are in a similar situation should be similarly taxed. However, it is also considered fair to charge motorists a fee for the right to use the roads, while exempting non-drivers – an example of a "user fee.'
- Income tax rates increase as taxable income increases, because the principle of "vertical equity" implies that it is fair to require those with a greater capacity to pay tax to bear relatively more of the total tax burden.
- A "carbon tax" would tax fossil fuels in proportion to the amount of carbon dioxide released to the atmosphere on combustion. The goal here is "intergenerational equity," since the accumulation of atmospheric carbon dioxide is believed to be responsible for the greenhouse effect and global warming. It is considered unfair for this generation to alter irrevocably the global climate in which future generations will have to live.
- School supplies are, in Nova Scotia, exempt from provincial sales tax. Reducing the tax barriers to education is seen as increasing "equality of opportunity," and thereby improving the equity of the process by which individuals gain income.

2 Taxation and the Overall Impact of Government

Canadians make their contributions to the financial health of government in a variety of ways. We pay sales tax on retail purchases, customs duties on imported goods, premiums to the Unemployment Insurance Commission, contributions to the Canada Pension Plan, and fees for licences and university tuition – as well as provincial and federal taxes on our income flows, and municipal taxes on our stock of real-estate wealth. The finances of the state benefit both from payments made directly to municipal, provincial, and federal government departments and from payments made to agencies of government (such as school boards) and nominally private organizations (such as hospitals and universities), whose funding is largely derived from public sources. The ways in which these payments are labelled and routed is not the issue – a comprehensive concept of taxation would include all payments made to agencies of government, or to non-commercial government-financed enterprises.

Furthermore, the equity of the tax system really cannot be considered in isolation from other policy decisions of government. Explicit transfer payments to individuals or firms appear as expenditure items in the national accounts, and the visibility of such transactions is partly responsible for the growth of invisible "tax expenditures," or conditional exemptions from taxation, which achieve the same redistribution of resources. In the area of personal income taxation, some tax exemptions have been recently converted to tax credits (for example, the deduction from taxable income for dependent children has been converted into a tax credit). If tax credits were made fully refundable, taxpayers with very low income would receive net payments from government. Indeed, many advocates of social policy reform have argued for a "negative income tax" in which transfer payments would be consciously integrated into the income tax system, since the current system of implicit taxation (i.e., the reduction in social assistance payments as earnings increase) can impose very high financial disincentives to increased labour supply.

In practice, the tax and transfer systems are inevitably closely linked – indeed, it can be argued that transfer payments are "negative taxes." The net impact of taxes and transfers on individuals is the difference between payments made to and payments received from government. This net impact is relevant for equity purposes. Although some tax sources (such as a value-added tax) may be regressive, taking a higher percentage of the income of the relatively poor, the tax/transfer system as a whole may be progressive, if expenditures benefit primarily the less affluent (as in Sweden). In Canada, redistribution between income classes had historically come largely from government expenditures, since aggregate taxation has often been found (e.g., see Gillespie 1980) to be roughly proportionate to income received over much of the income range.

As well, governments often have to choose between the use of tax or transfer incentives and the use of regulation or other policies as a means of achieving desired social objectives. The fairness of a given tax system must be considered relative to the fairness of available alternative policy decisions. One can cite many examples, from the taxation or regulation of polluters to the choice between tariffs or import controls, but anti-inflation policy is a particularly important instance.

In the 1970s, proposals for a "tax-based incomes policy" (TIP) were based on the idea that taxing increases in money wages and profits in excess of a statutory norm would discourage inflationary price increases. By many criteria of equity, a TIP would have been an unfair tax. This fact was widely recognized, and may be part of the reason why the TIP was never adopted. However, inflation also produces a redistribution of real resources between individuals, which many believe to be unfair. In the 1980s, the restrictive monetary policy that has, in fact, been used to contain inflation has also produced record unemployment, whose burden is unfairly distributed in the population. The fairness of a tax-based incomes policy has, therefore, to be considered relative to the fairness of alternative policy choices – either to let inflation continue to accelerate or to impose restrictive demand-management policies, at the cost of increased unemployment.

In short, taxation is an important part of the impact government has on society, but it is only a part. The equity (however conceived) of economic outcomes depends on all the decisions of government: demand management, spending, regulation, and taxation. It would be a mistake to emphasize fairness in taxation in isolation from the fairness of other policy decisions, or at the expense of all other considerations. However fair or unfair the tax system is, other policy decisions of government can either negate or accentuate its fairness.

3 The "Sometimes" Existence of Trade-offs

Since this paper has already discussed alternative policy instruments of government and will shortly consider alternative concepts of fairness, a word of caution is in order. The opening chapter of most introductory economics textbooks presents a diagram, like figure 1 here, in which a society is portrayed as being at a point, such as B, and the curved line is a "production possibility frontier," which is used to represent the idea that more of good X can be had only at the cost of consuming less of good Y. Like ducklings hatching from the egg, fledgling economists often imprint on the first thing they see, and continue throughout their professional lives to focus instinctively on the idea of "trade-offs."

However, despite the habitual reflex that leads some to speak of a trade-off between "equity" and "efficiency,"[1] the very same individ-

Figure 1

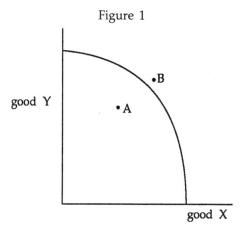

good Y

good X

uals can sometimes be heard complaining about the inefficiencies of economic life, perhaps induced by government activity, which implies necessarily that society is at a point, such as A, i.e., not on the production possibility frontier. If there are inefficiencies in the utilization of economic resources, whether from the failure of markets or of governments, it is possible to obtain more of both desired goods. In the best of all possible worlds, there would be no such inefficiencies, and society would necessarily have to trade off more of good X for less of good Y, as at point B in figure 1. In the second-best world in which we actually live, however, there are many dimensions to economic life, and many sources of productive inefficiency.

It may be the case, for example, that sometimes there is a trade-off to be made between "horizontal equity" and some other dimension of equity. But it may also be the case that countries with more uniform tax codes have more efficient capital markets (because the allocation of capital is determined by economic productivity, rather than by tax incentives). If so, the greater "horizontal equity" will promote greater efficiency in the allocation of capital, and a more productive bequest of capital to succeeding generations. The habitual reflex of economists is to talk of "policy trade-offs," but one should not allow this reflex to replace the hard work of careful analysis of inefficiencies in the real world.

4 Time and Fairness

Fairness in taxation has a time dimension, because social values and social realities change over time, because economic processes may counteract inequities in taxation over time, and because the calculation and payment of taxes over time create significant practical and perceptual difficulties for the attainment of "fairness."

If social values changed only in degree, and not in kind, the issue of tax equity would be simpler. If, for example, social preferences for equality of family income were weaker in the 1980s and stronger in the 1990s, it would be straightforward to change tax rates to achieve the desired degree of income redistribution. However, changes in social values can also be more profound, and the very concept of "family income" can become problematic.

In 1966, the Royal Commission on Taxation argued that the incomes of all family members should be aggregated and taxed as a unit. The social context for this recommendation was a society dominated by single-earner households, in which gender discrimination was quite acceptable. It was, for example, considered fair for minimum-wage law in Ontario to specify different minimum wages for men and women (in 1964, $1.00 per hour for men, and $0.85 per hour for women). Over the past 25 years, the labour force participation rate of married women has increased dramatically and the social acceptability of discrimination has decreased even more dramatically. The adoption of a family income base for taxation implies that the tax paid on an additional $1.00 of female earnings will depend on the amount of male income. The current debate as to whether this is "fair," or not, is very different from that engaged in in the 1960s.

The passage of time may also serve to counteract inequities in the current administration of taxation, because past inequities can become capitalized in current asset prices. It would be clearly unfair, for example, for a municipality to decrease property taxes for houses on the south side of every street. However, if a municipality did so, it would not take long before southern houses sold for more than northern houses in the real-estate market. The tax differential between southern and northern houses would become capitalized into housing prices (thereby benefiting the initial owners), but in equilibrium those who buy houses on either the north or the south side of a street will bear the same net total cost for housing. Once tax differentials are capitalized into asset prices, removing a tax break penalizes the current owners of capitalized assets, because they paid a price that reflected the expectation of continued favourable tax treatment – and they are likely to see the loss of their tax break as "unfair."

As the Meade Report (Institute for Fiscal Studies 1978, 14) argued: "From the point of view of 'horizontal equity' there is thus some truth to the view that 'an old tax is a good tax' but ... a committee which is set up to consider possible improvements in a tax structure can hardly take as a working rule that whatever exists, simply because it exists, necessarily constitutes the best of all possible worlds." However, it is essential to consider which inequities of the tax system may already have been capitalized into differential asset prices when considering the equity of reforms to the current tax system.

Assessment of tax liabilities is one thing, but payment is another, and as the saying goes, "a tax deferred is a tax avoided." As well, although individuals may remain unchanged over time, the composition of families and of voluntary organizations is not necessarily stable. When the composition of tax-paying units changes, tax authorities have to be able to attribute equitably the tax liability of the unit to its underlying membership, while also avoiding the establishment of tax incentives to the artificial creation or dissolution of families and organizations.

There is always a time dimension to the administration of a tax system, since the taxation of a transaction (such as a retail sale) depends on when it is deemed to occur, whereas the taxation of a flow (such as income) depends on the specification of a time period of measurement and the taxation of a stock (such as wealth) depends on the assessment of its value at a particular date. In an inflationary environment, the measuring-rod of money values changes over time, creating particular problems for the taxation of the real value of capital gains and the real return on interest payments.

In an inflationary environment, money income received as interest payments is only in part a real return on capital owned – part is also compensation for the erosion by inflation of the real value of principal owned. If all interest received is taxed as income, inflation implies partial taxation of wealth, as well as of income. This may be seen as unfair, but it would also be very difficult to maintain the perception of equity in income taxation if part of interest income were exempt from tax, while all of labour income were subject to tax. Inflation implies, in general, that equal dollar values at the various times at which tax liabilities are calculated and then paid do not correspond to equal real values. The pursuit of both actual equity in flows of real resources and perceived equity in measured money values then becomes extremely difficult.

5 Horizontal Equity

The principle of "horizontal equity" requires that similar tax-paying units should pay similar taxes, but to make this principle operational one must define the tax-paying unit and specify the criteria of similarity. In personal income taxation, the tax-paying unit may be defined as the individual or the family. Similarity of such units may be defined in terms of similarity of ability to pay (wealth or income or consumption), similarity of need, similar degree of use of public services, or similar personal characteristics such as citizenship. All these definitional choices depend upon an underlying idea of fairness.

Some taxes (such as the retail sales tax) are inherently taxes paid by the individual purchaser, but there has long been a debate on whether it should be families or individuals who pay income or wealth taxes. In 1966, the Royal Commission on Taxation argued that "in most families incomes are pooled, consumption is collective and responsibilities are shared. It should be an objective of the tax system to reflect this fact by considering families as taxable units. The ability to pay of the family, as distinct from the individual members of the family, must be recognized" (10). Advocacy of family income taxation combines an ethical statement about "ability to pay" as a criterion of tax equity with an empirical statement about social reality, i.e., the actual degree of pooling of income and consumption within families.

How much inequality is there within families? Is it any concern of the state? In the 1960s, intrafamily inequality was presumed to be minimal, and there may have been, in addition, an attitude that state decision making should not intrude upon the sphere of family life. In the 1990s there is a greatly increased consciousness of social and economic inequalities within families and a recognition that taxes and transfers typically do alter the intrafamily distribution of economic resources (see Apps and Rees 1988). Unfortunately, however, in both the 1960s and the 1990s there is very little reliable empirical evidence on the precise degree of inequality in the intrafamily allocation of resources (Gronau's 1991 article is an example of recent literature).

There is one model of family behaviour and one type of tax system in which the distinction between families and individuals does not matter. In Becker's (1981) theory of the family, the altruistic/dictatorial family patriarch optimally allocates the total resources of the family among family members. Differing tax rates may affect the supply of paid labour of various family members, but not the final distribution of consumption. However, as a descriptive model of social reality, this picture has always been of questionable legitimacy – as well as being normatively offensive to many people.

Alternatively, if income tax were a fixed percentage of all income, with no deductions or exemptions, it would make no difference to families whether the family or the individual was defined as the tax-paying unit, since the total tax bill would be identical. However, a purely proportional income tax would conflict with the ideal of "vertical equity," i.e., progressive tax rates that increase with greater ability to pay.

Despite increasing instability of the family unit, the social reality is that most Canadians continue to live in families that provide for many of their most important needs. In addition to their private command over market income and wealth, individuals do have claims on other family members, for both non-marketed goods and services (which are untaxed) and financial transfers. Currently, non-market cash transfers between family members are sometimes taxed and sometimes not. Gifts and inheritances are not taxed as income in the hands of recipients, but alimony and child-support payments are considered taxable income of the recipient (and are deductible from the taxable income of the paying spouse). The taxation of alimony and child-support payments is an illustration of the complexity of the interaction of taxation rules and social institutions since similar cash transfers made within an intact family would not be taxed as income of the recipient. Although the total tax payable by an intact family is greater than the tax payable by a split family (since support payments are deductible from the taxable income of the higher-income separated spouse), the lower-income separated spouse bears a larger share of the total tax burden. A fair-tax commission cannot ignore the complexities introduced by these social realities, or their fiscal implications.

The argument for a purely individualistic tax system is partly ethical (that individuals should be treated as individuals) and partly empirical. How large is intrafamily inequality compared with interfamily inequality? Real inequalities within the family will be measurable only by differences in personal money incomes if collective family consumption (e.g., the amenities of housing) is relatively small and if intrafamily transfers of resources are minimal. However, family expenditure data indicate that neither statement is particularly realistic. And one must remember that interfamily inequality in Canada is quite large – the average income of the top 20 per cent of families is approximately 6.5 times greater than the average income of the bottom 20 per cent of families – hence the degree of interfamily inequality is considerably greater than any reasonable estimate of the degree of intrafamily inequality. For this reason, those who are primarily concerned with greater equality of consumption tend to remain convinced of the merits of family income as a base for income tax and for transfer policy.

Given the definition of the tax-paying unit, one criterion for "horizontal equity" is that those with an equal ability to pay should pay a similar amount of tax – but what is "ability to pay"? Some discussions of taxation appear to be based, at least implicitly, on the idea that "ability to pay" is really about the utility taxpayers receive, after the payment of tax. Although economists typically assume that utility is non-comparable, there are some allowances made for "need" in tax administration. The Income Tax Act allows us to deduct medical expenses, and the Carter Report advocated that, in general, the tax system should recognize "special responsibilities and non-discretionary expenditures." The implicit idea is that people with these needs derive less utility from a given income and hence should pay less tax.

However, economies of scale in household operation (such as the sharing of rent or other fixed expenses) also imply that individuals who cohabit with others derive greater utility from a given flow of money income, and are therefore "able" to pay more tax. Individuals who enjoy their work have more utility, after taxation, than do similar people who hate their jobs. Although some researchers (e.g., Kapetyn, van de Geer, and van de Stadt 1985) have tried to use polling data to measure the subjective burden of taxation, "equal sacrifice" is not a practical ideal for the tax system.

It is ultimately the subjective burden of taxation that matters, both for behaviour and for well-being, but it is neither feasible nor desirable to use "utility" as a measure of ability to pay. If taxpayers knew that their own reports of the pain of tax payments might affect their tax liabilities, one might reasonably expect their squeals of anguish to mount in volume, to dramatic heights. As well as being impractical, it is also unethical to use actual individual well-being as the criterion of "ability to pay." It is hard to argue that individuals with expensive tastes should be taxed more lightly because their personal-subsistence standards are more expensive or, equivalently, that those with low consumption expectations should pay more tax.

However, if actual subjective individual well-being cannot be the basis for assessing tax-paying ability, what should be? Advocates of consumption taxation argue that those who withdraw more from the social stock of available goods and services have greater ability to pay tax. Critics note that taxation of consumption, rather than income, implies that savings are not taxed (at least, until they are spent). Individuals have control over whether income is saved or consumed;

hence, income is a better measure of the change over time in an individual's potential command over goods and services. By this criterion, those with equal ability to pay are those with equal incomes. However, if income is defined as "the maximum value a person can consume during a period and still be as well off (as wealthy) at the end of the period as he was at the beginning" (Hicks 1946, 75), wealth still remains. An individual's wealth is his or her total potential stock of command over goods and services at a particular time – it can be argued that those with "equal ability to pay" should be thought of as those individuals with an equal stock of wealth.

The social reality is that individuals and relatively low incomes consume most of it, while wealth and high income are positively correlated. As a result, arguments about "vertical equity" are the subtext for this debate on how to define "horizontal equity." Moreover, one should not think of any of these concepts of the tax base as easy to administer in practice. We have the most experience at trying to define "income" for tax purposes (which is, in itself, a good reason for keeping income as the tax base), but "consumption" is at least as ambiguous a concept, and "wealth" has a number of alternative definitions, in practice.[2]

Given the definition of tax-paying units and the tax base, one must also face the fact that, in Canada, government operates at several levels – municipal, provincial, and federal. In a purely unitary state, there would be a single tax schedule for all parts of the country and a single level of provision of all public services. However, when subnational and subprovincial jurisdictions provide public services and set their own tax rates, an equal rate of tax may not be horizontally equitable. If, for example, schools are financed from local property taxes, an equal rate of tax would imply that towns with greater total assessment could finance better schools than could towns with smaller local assessment. Families with rich neighbours, and those who live in towns with a substantial commercial real-estate base, would receive greater net benefits from government than those who live in poor areas – even if they paid the same rate of tax.

Horizontal equity can be maintained if tax revenue is redistributed between jurisdictions – as in school financing within provinces and in federal-provincial equalization transfers between provinces. As section 36 (2) of the Constitution Act, 1982, puts it, the purpose of equalization payments is to ensure that individuals receive "reasonably comparable levels of public services at reasonably comparable levels of taxation." The general point is that, in a non-unitary state, "horizontal equity" requires financial transfers between jurisdictions to compensate for the differences between jurisdictions in taxable capacity.

In thinking of the "similarity" of taxpayers, fairness implies that some characteristics can be considered, but not others. Canadians would consider it grossly unfair, for example, if assessed taxable capacity under income tax were reduced for the adherents of some religions, but not others. It is equally clear that gender or race discrimination is considered unfair. However, it is considered fair for churches to escape property taxes, and Canadians do not appear to consider all ascriptive criteria to be irrelevant for tax purposes. Attitudes vary as to whether it is legitimate to discriminate in the taxation of non-resident foreigners, either directly as individuals or indirectly as shareholders in multinational corporations. As well, the Income Tax Act does now specify a tax deduction for those aged over 65. The presence of such features of the current tax system forces us to ask ourselves on what non-economic grounds it is fair to distinguish between tax-paying units.

6 User Fees

Ability to pay may be measured by consumption, income, or wealth, but in all these instances, horizontal equity is thought of as the idea that individuals with similar "ability to pay" should pay a similar amount of tax. An alternative basis for the idea of tax fairness is the idea of "fair exchange." If individuals use services provided by government, equity might be construed as requiring similar payments from individuals making a similar degree of use of government-provided services. "User fees" are, in fact, very common in Ontario, in areas from motor-vehicle licensing to the paying of university tuition. Such fees are occasionally differentiated somewhat among users (as in lower tuition fees for senior citizens), perhaps based on the implicit idea that the favoured group has lower incomes, and a lower-dollar price for that user group may still reflect a similar degree of personal sacrifice.

Nevertheless, it is more normal for user fees to be equal-dollar charges for all the consumers using a public service. Although there is a grey area of special fees for incremental services (e.g., the extra charge for a private hospital room), it is hard to make a general case that user fees are more "voluntary" than other forms of taxation.

As always, the degree to which an action is "voluntary" depends on the attractiveness of available alternative possible actions. Although one can escape buying a driver's licence by not driving and one can avoid paying university tuition by not going to university, one could also escape customs duties by consuming only domestic goods and it is possible to avoid paying income tax by becoming a subsistence farmer. The attractiveness of not driving depends, in part, on the quality of available public transportation, and the attractiveness of buying only domestically produced goods depends on how close they are to imports in price and quality. The quality of one's options determines the "voluntariness" of a tax. User fees can discourage frivolous use and/or wastage of publicly provided services, but whether they can be typified as a "voluntary" tax depends on the facts of the issue.

Moreover, fundamentally the fairness of the criterion of "fair exchange" as a general rule depends upon the fairness of the original distribution of income and wealth. After all, the fair exchange of a dollar's worth of commodity for a dollar in cash will leave both rich and poor where they initially were in total-wealth terms – the issue of vertical equity will remain unaddressed.

In contemplating user charges for public services, it is also worth recalling why these services are publicly provided and subsidized. Bus fares are subsidized in Canada because it is cheaper and less polluting to subsidize public transit than to build vast networks of superhighways for the individual automobile commuter. Education is subsidized because a more educated citizenry is a productive resource for the economy as a whole. Public provision of services is often motivated by the externalities that consumption of these services entails – the whole point of public provision, and the efficiencies it generates for a society as a whole, are lost if user fees are required to cover the total cost of operation.

7 Vertical Equity

To put it plainly, the principle underlying "vertical equity" is that the rich should pay more tax than the poor, because they can afford to. By this criterion, one of the objectives of the tax system should be to progressively increase tax rates as ability to pay increases so that the distribution of after-tax income will become more equal. To this end, in the 1950s and 1960s it was common to observe a very high rate of nominal taxation on upper-income groups – but some cynicism was also in order. As the Carter Report commented, "the top marginal rate is now about 80%, and applies to income in excess of $400,000. In our opinion, rates as high as this are on the statute books only because they are readily avoided by most of the few people with incomes of this size" (1966, 21). Their own recommendation was for a reduction in the top marginal tax rate to something less than 50 per cent and a comprehensive reform of the myriad of tax-avoidance techniques, which implied that the average effective tax rate on the extremely wealthy was in fact no higher than for those with much lower incomes. Subsequently, this theme – of broadening the base of income tax while decreasing top marginal rates – has been picked up in a number of other countries (see Head, this volume). However, although it is clear that marginal tax rates of upper-income groups have been cut substantially, it is not so clear that a substantial number of tax-avoidance techniques do not remain.

As had already been noted, the definition of the tax base and the tax-paying unit interact with the issue of vertical equity. In a progressive income tax system, the aggregation of two small individual incomes into a larger family income will imply an increase in tax liability. Similarly, if the objective is to tax consumption, taxes administered at the point of sale (like the retail sales tax or the goods and services tax) will constitute a constant percentage of all consumer expenditure, but since the savings of upper-income groups will escape taxation altogether, upper-income groups will pay a smaller percentage of their income in tax than will lower-income groups.

However, the taxation of consumption could be made progressive if consumption were defined as income minus registered savings and if a progressive rate of taxation were applied to consumption, thus defined. Although the current tax treatment of Registered Retirement Savings Plans (RRSPs) goes part of the way to converting our income tax into a consumption tax of this type, the administration of a full-fledged progressive consumption tax has all the administrative difficulties of an income tax, plus the capital-market distortions and administrative complexities of policing the flow of savings.

Although it can be argued that the ultimate basis of individual well-being is lifetime command over resources, it is not feasible to use lifetime income as the tax base. After all, by the time it is known what an individual's total lifetime income actually is, it is too late for taxation. Income flows must necessarily be taxed on a shorter-period basis, and our customary accounting period has been annual. One must recognize, however, that a progressive tax on annual income implies some redistribution in consumption over the life cycle (compared to a proportional tax) since the lower-income years of youth and retirement attract a relatively low rate of income taxation, compared to the peak-earnings years of middle age. At any time, therefore, a progressive tax on annual income means that the middle-aged tend to pay more tax – a situation that might be seen as unfair in any given year, but is perfectly equitable from a life-cycle perspective.

In addition to predictable changes in income over the life cycle, individuals face random, year-to-year variations in their income flows. The tax system enables individuals to smooth out such variability in income flows by income averaging, by allowing the offset of capital gains and losses, and by permitting the limited "parking" of income in RRSP's. More fundamentally, in the tax/transfer system as a whole, the state is a "co-adventurer" in the fortunes of individual taxpayers. Governments share in the gains of individuals through progressive taxation, but the state also mitigates any losses that occur, through a declining tax rate in income tax and the possibility of social assistance. To some degree, therefore, one can justify a progressive annual income tax and social assistance on efficiency grounds, since their absence would imply that risk-averse individuals would tend to "play it safe" even if, on average, there were a net gain from risk taking.

However, the most important reason for progressive income taxation is undoubtedly the moral value of greater equality – but this has never been seen as an absolute value. It has long been recognized that a tax system which aimed at absolute equality would produce equal poverty, since absolute equality can be produced only by confiscating all above-average incomes. As Dalton (1935, 21) noted: "The rejection of crude egalitarianism does not take us far, though there are some who seem to think that, when they have disposed of the argument for absolute equality, they have disposed also of all arguments for reducing existing inequalities."

However, what is "greater equality"? Although it is easy to say that more for the poor and less for the rich means more equality, the real world is not composed of only two income classes. Once one allows for the fact that the tax system may redistribute resources both between the rich and the middle class and between the middle class and the poor, the concept of "equality" becomes much more ambiguous.[3]

Table 1 presents an illustrative calculation of tax choices in a society in which 20 per cent of the population is rich, 60 per cent is middle class, and 20 per cent is poor. It assumes that this society has to find some way of financing a total tax burden equal to 23 per cent of pre-tax income, and presents two stark alternatives.[4] In Tax Regime 1, all tax revenue is raised by taxation on the middle class; in Tax Regime 2, all individuals pay exactly the same proportion of their income in tax. Which tax regime produces a more equal distribution of after-tax income? Which tax regime is "fairer"?

TABLE 1
An Illustrative Tax Policy Choice

	Rich	Middle	Poor
Number	20	60	20
Pre-tax income	84,000	60,000	8,400
Pre-tax income share	30.8%	66.1%	3.1%
Tax regime 1			
Tax rate	0	0.35	0
After-tax income	84,000	39,000	8,400
After-tax income share	40%	56%	4%
Tax regime 2			
Tax rate	0.231	0.231	0.231
After-tax income	64,580	46,120	6,460
After-tax income share	30.8%	66.1%	3.1%

The numbers in table 1 were picked so that the after-tax income shares of the population under Tax Regime 1 would roughly correspond with the actual distribution of money income among Canadian families and unattached individuals in recent years. Under Tax Regime 1, where the middle class pays all the taxes, the richest 20 per cent of the population is better off, but so is the poorest 20 per cent. If one judges fairness solely by what happens to the well-being of the poorest members of society (as advocated by Green [1992]), then Tax Regime 1 produces a fairer distribution of after-tax income. However, some might also regard as "fair" the idea that all individuals pay the same percentage of their income in tax, as in Tax Regime 2, despite the fact that this implies that the poorest 20 per cent of the population gets less income, after tax.

Table 1 is not intended to suggest that the tax system has only these two choices. Presumably, the job of a fair-tax commission is to design a tax system that is better than either a flat tax, or one that "soaks the middle class." Table 1 is intended to suggest that there are fundamental ambiguities in the measurement of economic inequality, and in the concept of tax fairness, which revolve around the relative importance placed on inequalities between each level of the income distribution – e.g., the inequalities between the very poorest and the middle class of society and between the middle class and the more affluent.

The difficult issue is the degree of tax progressivity that best expresses society's balancing of the values of personal liberty, greater social equality, and growth/capital accumulation for future generations. Economics cannot specify such values. Economic theory can provide abstract models of optimal-taxation regimes, although such models are often highly stylized. Econometric analysis can dispose of some myths about the impact of taxation (for example, it is not true that higher income taxes imply substantial declines in hours of paid labour supply). Economics can also emphasize the constraints that the migration of labour imposes on the feasible policies of subnational jurisdictions within a national labour market and the problems posed by capital mobility in global financial markets. It is, however, in the political arena that the problem of vertical equity is invariably "solved."

8 Intergenerational Equity

Fairness and equity are central to the discussion of intergenerational issues because power is so unavoidably unequal. This generation can affect the welfare of future generations by running down the capital stock, or by despoiling the environment, but there is nothing future generations can do to us. Our decisions, individual and collective, are necessarily shaped by our norms of "fairness" in intergenerational distribution, and many of the decisions made by this generation will affect the welfare of future generations. Specific taxes (such as the proposed carbon tax) can help to shift consumption and production away from environmentally damaging processes. Specific features of the corporate tax system (such as accelerated depreciation) can improve incentives for investment in plant and equipment, and specific changes in individual taxation may encourage saving (e.g., a shift to consumption taxation rather than income taxation). Specific transfers (such as family allowance or social assistance) will influence the health and skills of vulnerable members of the next generation. And not only will particular taxes affect capital formation, the aggregate tax burden will also affect the rate of economic growth and aggregate capital formation. Furthermore, if taxes are insufficient to cover government expenditure, an increasing deficit will burden future generations of taxpayers with debt repayment.

The bequest of the current generation to future generations is composed of:

- a physical capital stock of plant, equipment, and public works;
- society's intangible stock of human capital in individual, productive skills, and its intellectual capital of research and technology;
- the quality of the natural environment;
- the social environment within which economic processes operate; and
- net financial indebtedness to foreign residents.

The physical capital stock accumulates over the generations as individuals decide to invest in housing and in directly productive capital, and as governments decide on the repair or renewal of public infrastructure. Human capital is accumulated as schools develop the skills of each new generation and as parents contribute to the education of their children. Both individually and collectively, we also make decisions with environmental implications for future generations – such as our decisions on the use of fossil or nuclear fuels. And all our economic decisions take place within, and depend upon, a framework of social institutions. The "social capital" of our society will erode over time to the extent that norms of social behaviour (e.g., of law-abidingness or of non-violent conflict resolution) break down or to the degree that the pressures on family life prevent the family from fulfilling its historic social functions of socialization, nurturance, and economic security.[5] The tax system influences all these processes. How much weight should be placed on each of the different components of intergenerational transfers? The aggregate value of intergenerational bequest is affected by taxation decisions, both in their detail and in aggregate. What is a fair allocation of aggregate resources between this generation and future generations?

There is one economic model in which government does not have to worry about intergenerational equity. Barro (1974) argued that, if individuals care altruistically about their descendants (who, in turn, cared about their own descendants), the issue of intergenerational equity is internalized, over generations, within families. If individuals recognize that a government deficit incurred today represents deferred taxation, these forward-looking, altruistic individuals will leave their descendants an increased bequest of private assets, in order to enable them to pay their future tax liabilities. In this scenario, government decisions to decrease taxes and increase deficits are offset by increased private savings – the net bequest to future generations always remains optimal.

If one does not accept this vision of reality (and most economists do not), intergenerational equity poses real problems. No longer can one divorce issues of equity and efficiency, since a tax structure that is inefficient in maximizing the rate of growth of aggregate output will bequeath a smaller capital stock to future generations. The total magnitude of taxation, relative to expenditure, becomes an equity issue, in the sense that deficits accumulate and become a debt burden on future generations. And since bequests to future generations come in a variety of forms, the effect of detailed aspects of taxation on the environment; on society's acquisition of human capital; on continued social cohesion; and on the continued accumulation of plant, equipment, and public works become dimensions of the issue of fairness in taxation.

9 Process Equity

One concept of fairness holds that an outcome is "fair" if it has occurred as the result of a process that is "fair."[6] Economic inequality, in this view, can occur only if economic processes are inequitable – hence, a fair-tax system is one that acts so as to maintain the fairness of economic processes and/or eliminate any unfairness in economic processes. Should a fair-tax system, therefore, differentiate on the basis of how income was acquired? The Carter Report argued, on grounds of both equity and administrative efficiency, that "a dollar is a dollar," and that, if the primary basis for taxation is to be income, the origin of such income is irrelevant for taxation purposes. Implicitly, this argument says that all the processes by which a dollar is acquired are of equal fairness. As well, the commission emphasized that differential taxation of income sources creates incentives to reclassify income flows (thereby increasing the administrative costs of the tax system) or to redirect economic resources to low-tax activities (thereby decreasing aggregate economic efficiency).

The perspective of the Carter Report was influential in persuading Canadian tax authorities to begin taxation of realized capital gains in 1971 – although initially at only half the rate applied to income from other sources. The tradition of special favourable treatment for capital gains continued with the 1985 introduction of a lifetime exemption of $500,000 in capital-gains income (later reduced to $100,000). Since income earned from labour, or by other means, has no similar lifetime exemption, the treatment of capital gains is horizontally inequitable. Since one has to have capital in order to have the possibility of making capital gains, the special tax treatment of capital gains benefits primarily the affluent, thereby contradicting the ideal of vertical equity.

However, appeals for unequal taxation may also be made on the grounds of process equity. A speculation tax on property developers has been discussed, partly motivated by a desire to check the inflation of housing prices, but partly also driven by the moral argument that it is unfair for some to make so much more by flipping properties than most individuals can make by continuous toil. Underlying this proposal is the idea is that the tax system should tax the utility gain of individuals, in the name of greater equality of sacrifice of utility. Since the worker gave up time and energy to earn money income, while the speculator did not, by the criterion of "equal sacrifice" it would be seen as fair to tax the speculator more heavily than the worker. However, another underlying idea is that speculative property gains are "illegitimately" acquired, in either or both of two senses. If land is in fixed supply, it can be argued that the activity of land speculation serves no legitimate public purpose. If real-estate profits are obtained by collusion and/or by manipulation of public officials (e.g., in zoning regulation), the market process may be seen as unfair. From either perspective, greater taxation of land-speculation profits may then be seen as improving the process equity of market forces.

More fundamentally, the taxation of inheritances raises the issue of the equality of opportunity, which is essential for the perceived process equity of a market economy. In contrast to most other nations, Canada does not currently have any inheritance or estate taxes,[7] since this tax field was deserted by the federal government in 1972 and thereafter destroyed by interprovincial tax competition. However, since the bequests received by an individual represent an increase in his or her command over economic resources, it would seem inconsistent with the principle of horizontal equity in income taxation that these bequests are not taxed as income. As well, the principle of equality of sacrifice would require higher taxes on bequests than on other income, since receipt of a bequest requires no exertion or risk from individuals.

If a capitalist economic system is a race for individual success, a basic norm of equity is that all individuals should start from approximately the same starting-line. Although it is well recognized that families differ in the magnitude of their investment in the education and training of their children, such inequalities in endowment of childhood human capital are mitigated by a broad program of public investment in children, ranging from subsidized day care to free public schools and subsidized post-secondary training. Furthermore, inequalities in non-financial parental transfers to children are orders of magnitude smaller than differentials in financial inheritances – one must remember that at the top of the Canadian wealth distribution sit a few multi-billionaire families, but at the bottom are the approximately 30 per cent of Canadian families with nil or negative assets (see Davies 1991).

10 Conclusion

Both in principle and in practice, equity in taxation cannot be one-dimensional. In principle, one cannot, as a philosophical matter, logically derive all existing ideas of fairness from a common underlying root. The idea of equity as whatever a fair process produces starts from a very different philosophical basis than the idea that one should judge directly the fairness of outcomes. A desire for equity between generations cannot be logically derived from the idea of "fair exchange" or from ideas of horizontal equity.

In practice, general philosophical premises must also be combined with a particular understanding of the nature of the real world if one is to draw practical conclusions. Even if one believes, for example, that process equity is all that matters, one's view of profits taxation will depend on whether or not one believes that profits are typically obtained "fairly" in competitive markets or "unfairly," by price fixing in oligopolistic markets.

In practice, individuals also typically believe simultaneously in a number of different concepts of fairness, and the tax systems of countries express a number of different dimensions of equity. One should not see this as irrational. Since each of these different ideas of equity is deep and complex, it is entirely reasonable for an individual to hold a number of views simultaneously, and work out their detailed interrelationship only as and when required. Of course, the members of a fair-tax commission are placed in a position where they are asked to work out all interactions (both equity and efficiency) of all taxes. However, they have the solace of knowing that, in the end, the weighting of the different dimensions of equity will inevitably be political, not logical. To some extent, political compromises within the commission will produce a report that does not reflect exactly any one individual's view of fairness, but is a composite of the views of all members. The political pressure of the interest groups outside the Fair Tax Commission will ultimately determine which parts of the report governments will adopt. However, a fair-tax commission can also make a real contribution by identifying those inefficiencies in the existing tax system that prevent the attainment of more of several objectives.

Moreover, in emphasizing one or another dimension of equity in taxation, one should not think of the tax system in isolation. The expenditure side of government is, for example, crucially important to "vertical equity." Indeed, precisely because the poor have so little to tax, variations in their tax rates are less important to them than the flows of public services and financial transfers they receive from government. In part, the Carter Report's emphasis on horizontal equity in taxation was derived from the belief that a non-distortionary tax system is likely to imply a higher rate of economic growth and a greater taxable capacity, from which public services and transfer payments can be financed. Such a perspective is also consistent with intergenerational equity, in the sense that faster economic growth implies a larger capital stock for future generations and increased ability to pay for the social programs that maintain our social cohesion, and the environmental programs that protect our natural heritage.

Notes

The first draft of this study was prepared for the Ontario Fair Tax Commission and was completed in February 1992. The comments of Allan Maslove, Shelley Phipps, and the participants in the workshop of the Fair Tax Commission, Toronto, 26 February 1992, have greatly assisted the revision process. Errors remaining are my own.

1 Usually it is very unclear what is meant by "equity" and "efficiency" in this supposed trade-off. This paper discusses the ambiguities in the idea of "equity" – see section 7 for a discussion of the ambiguities in "equality."

2 Should "wealth" include the present value of future pension receipts? Should it include the capitalized value of future royalties or earnings? For a discussion see Wolff (1991).

3 It has long been recognized (see Atkinson 1970) that ambiguities in the comparison of income distributions are very common – and these ambi-

guities are yet another reason for distrusting the cliché of an "equality/ efficiency" trade-off. In technical terms, one can compare income distributions by plotting their "Lorenz curves" (which graph the total percentage of income received by the poorest X per cent of the population). If these curves never cross, then in one population the poorest X per cent always receives more of total income, whatever X is, and relative inequality is unambiguously clear. However, in the real world, it is common for Lorenz curves to cross, frequently more than once, implying that the answer to the question of whether the poor receive more depends upon who the poor are defined to be. See Davies and Hoy (1991).

4 To keep the calculation simple, table 1 assumes that raising and spending tax revenue does not imply any change in the pre-tax distribution of income. Allowing public expenditure to affect the pre-tax income distribution or accounting for the influence of changing tax rates on individual behaviour (e.g., savings or labour supply) only increases the potential complexity, and ambiguity, of the situation.

5 These ideas are developed further in Osberg (1992).

6 As Green (this volume, p. 95) points out, libertarian philosophers such as Nozick (1974) have used this argument as a defence of existing property rights, but the argument also implies that the tainted past of wealth acquisition (e.g., the acquisition of land titles in North America) deprives the current distribution of property ownership of moral legitimacy.

7 Some assets can be rolled over, untaxed, to other family members, but the capital gains on most assets are deemed to be realized on the asset holder's death. This is best seen as ending the deferral of taxation on unrealized capital gains.

Bibliography

Apps, P.F., and R. Rees. 1988. "Taxation and the Household." *Journal of Public Economics*, 35: 355–69

Atkinson, A.B. 1970. "On the Measurement of Inequality." *Journal of Economic Theory*, 2: 244–63

Barro, Robert J. 1974. "Are Government Bonds Net Wealth?" *Journal of Political Economy*, 82 (6): 1095–1130

Becker, Gary S. 1981. *A Treatise on the Family*. Cambridge, MA: Harvard University Press

Canada. Royal Commission on Taxation. 1966. *Report* (Carter Report). Vols. 1 and 2. Ottawa: Queen's Printer

Carter Report. *See* Canada, Royal Commission on Taxation

Comanor, W.S., and R.H. Smiley. 1975. "Monopoly and the Distribution of Wealth." *Quarterly Journal of Economics*, 89: 177–94

Dalton, H. 1935. *Some Aspects of Inequality of Incomes in Modern Communities*. New York: E.F. Dutton

Davies, James. 1991. "The Distributive Effects of Wealth Taxes." *Canadian Public Policy*, 17 (3): 279–308

Davies, James, and M. Hoy. 1991. "Making Inequality Comparisons When Lorenz Curves Intersect." University of Western Ontario, Discussion Paper no. 1991–12, Mimeo. London, ON

Gillespie, W.I. 1980. *The Redistribution of Income in Canada*, Carleton Library no. 124. Toronto: Gage

Gronau, R. 1991. "The Intra-Family Allocation of Goods – How to Separate the Adult from the Child." *Journal of Labour Economics*, 9 (3): 207–35

Hicks, J.R. 1946. "Income." In *Readings in the Concept and Measurement of Income*, ed. R.H. Parker and G.C. Harcourt, 74–82. Cambridge: Cambridge University Press

Institute for Fiscal Studies. 1978. *The Structure and Reform of Direct Taxation: Report of a Committee Chaired by Prof. J.E. Meade* (Meade Report). London: Allen and Unwin

Kapetyn, A., S. van de Geer, and H. van de Stadt. 1985. "The Impact of Changes in Income and Family Composition on Subjective Measures of Well-Being." In *Horizontal Equity, Uncertainty and Economic Well-Being*, ed. M. David and T. Smeeding, 35–64. Chicago: University of Chicago Press

Kotlikoff, L. 1988. "Intergenerational Transfers and Savings." *The Journal of Economic Perspectives*, 2 (2): 41–58

Kotlikoff, L., and L. Summers. 1981. "The Role of Intergenerational Transfers in Aggregate Capital Accumulation." *Journal of Political Economy*, 89 (4): 706–32

Meade Report. *See* Institute for Fiscal Studies

Nozick, R. 1974. *Anarchy, State and Utopia*. New York: Basic Books

Osberg, Lars. 1992. "Substainable Social Development." In *Economic Policy: The Failure of Conservatism*, ed. Gideon Rosenbluth. Vancouver, BC: New Star Publishers (forthcoming)

Perry, J.H. 1989. *A Fiscal History of Canada – The Post War Years*. Canadian Taxpayer Paper no. 85. Toronto: Canadian Tax Foundation

Wolff, E.N. 1991. "The Distribution of Household Wealth: Methodological Issues, Time Trends and Cross-sectional Comparisons." In *Economic Inequality and Poverty: International Perspectives*, ed. L. Osberg, 92–133. Armonk, NY: M.E. Sharpe

3 Concepts of Equity in Taxation

LESLIE GREEN

In this paper, I explore, from the point of view of a moral and political philosopher, some general issues about the concept of equity or fairness in taxation. I argue, first, that one familiar notion of "equity" as employed in traditional public-finance literature is unhelpful for the policy maker and, second, that among apparently divergent political philosophies there is none the less a surprising consensus about the legitimacy of redistributive taxation.

The Primacy of Fairness

A tax system can properly be expected to fulfil a number of economic goals: it should secure a sufficient level of revenue for the government; play a role in stabilization policy; make efficient use of resources; and be easily administrable. We may also have somewhat more abstract political expectations for it: we may want it to express a common citizenship and mutual regard for one another; we may want it to help unify the nation. And, of course, we want it to be fair, equitable, and just.

Unfortunately, there is no good reason to think that all these goals can be maximized simultaneously. So how should we deal with conflicts among them? We might define thresholds of satisfaction. If the tax system cannot be completely efficient, we can at least require that it not be grossly inefficient; if it cannot maximize revenue, it should provide at least an adequate level; and so on. But having in this way made our expectations more modest, conflicts are none the less likely to remain, so we have no option but to set our aims in some order of priority.

With respect to tax reform, we should endorse the priority suggested by Canada's Royal Commission on Taxation (1966, 4), namely, that "the first and most essential purpose of taxation is to share the burden of the state fairly among all individuals and families. Unless the allocation of the burden is generally accepted as fair, the social and political fabric of a country is weakened and can be destroyed ... scrupulous fairness in taxation must override all other objectives where there is a conflict among objectives." It is interesting that this view accords so closely with a more general thesis about the priority of justice, defended by one of the most influential English-speaking political philosophers. John Rawls (1971, 4) contends: "Justice is the first virtue of social institutions, as truth is of systems of thought. A theory however elegant and economical must be rejected or revised if it is untrue; likewise laws and institutions no matter how efficient and well-arranged must be reformed or abolished if they are unjust ... The only thing that permits us to acquiesce in an erroneous theory is the lack of a better one; analogously, an injustice is tolerable only when it is necessary to avoid an even greater injustice." This crystallizes a deep view about the role of justice in moral and political theory: it is the dominant and structuring virtue of social institutions. But there are also more humble reasons for giving priority to justice in tax reform. People will try to avoid and evade taxes they believe to be unfair, and no tax system can survive without a substantial measure of voluntary compliance.

But, if this is so, what can moral or political theory contribute to our understanding of tax fairness? After all, if we are concerned with voluntary compliance and the stability that results from it, it might seem that we should do sociology instead of philosophy. We should survey people to find out what they believe fairness in tax to be and then strive to make the system conform to that rather than to some abstract ideal that can only give rise to disagreement.

One critic of the Carter Report (Robinson 1967, 8) voiced such a view, writing that "equity in taxation is relative, and involves a subjective judgement as to what is fair and just, which is in turn a judgement about whether a particular state of affairs conforms to tacit but generally accepted rules of business and society." But, whatever it means for a distribution of economic resources to be "fair and just," it is not the generally accepted rules of business and society since they themselves may be unjust and may conflict with each other.

Moreover, there is a real question as to whether we could even uncover people's sincere views about fairness in this way. First and obviously, self-interest gives an incentive to misrepresent one's views about tax fairness. Deciding how to respond to such a survey question, like revealing one's level of demand for a public good, involves strategic reasoning. Second, one of the things we do believe about political ideals like fairness is that they are open to challenge by logic, evidence, and principle. We do not, in fact, want our views to become policy if we come to think they are mistaken. So there is just no way for the policy maker to avoid judgements about what fairness really requires.

But what then are we to make of disagreements over the very meaning of such terms as "equity" and "fairness"? Conceptual disputes in the social sciences arise in different ways. Some are attributable to equivocation or ambiguity, in the way "bank" is ambiguous, as meaning both the side of a river and a place to keep money. Others result from the irremediable vagueness of terms used, such as "bald" and "short," which are without bright boundaries. If this were all there was to the problem, then we could proceed by stipulating clear, if arbitrary, definitions. Too much writing in tax policy is marred by the assumption that such a solution will do. It will not, however, because there is a deeper issue. Some disputes arise, not from vagueness or ambiguity, but from the fact than many political concepts are value-charged. To call a tax system "fair" is not just to describe it; it is to praise and recommend it. And because the criteria by which we judge such a system are complex and competing, we are likely to end up with competing views about what fairness really is. Political theorists have called such notions "essentially contested concepts" (Connolly 1974). They have the feature that debates about what "equity" and "justice" really mean are political debates, not debates about grammar or evidence. So judgements about principles are unavoidable.

Horizontal and Vertical Equity

There is no real consistency with respect to the use of the terms "equity," "fairness," and "justice" in tax theory. Some writers drift from one to the other, using them as if they were interchangeable; others insist somewhat arbitrarily on making distinctions among them. But one usage has become entrenched. Drawing on a distinction popularized by R.A. Musgrave (1959, 15), formulated by Pigou (1928, 8,

60) but present all the way back to Aristotle, many writers distinguish between horizontal equity – the equal reatment of people who are equally situated – and vertical equity – the appropriately different treatment of people who are differently situated.

The tradition regards these as distinct aspects or kinds of equity. It also holds that horizontal equity is in some way clearer and more easily attained than is vertical equity. Charles M. Allan (1971, 37) is representative in this respect:

> Two classes of equity are distinguished. The first, horizontal equity, describes the equal treatment of equal people. This principle is unchallengeable as an ideal and is not impracticable of operation. People of equal incomes, for example, might be required to pay the same income taxes. All people who smoke twenty cigarettes per day would be required to pay the same in specific tobacco taxes. The second class is vertical equity, which describes the treatment of taxpayers who are unequal with the appropriate degree of inequality. While vertical equity also has great merit as an ideal, it is very hard to achieve in practice. This is because there are so many views as to what is the appropriate degree of inequality.

Similarly, Richard A. Musgrave (1987, 114) reports that most economists think that "the horizontal aspects of equity (or, at least, certain parts thereof) can be dealt with, while the vertical phase had better be left to the softer field of social ethics."

I wish to explore this notion that horizontal equity is in some way firmer than vertical equity, for I think it reveals something significant about one way the concept of equity is often used by tax theorists. Horizontal equity requires "the equal treatment of equal people." Now, "equal" is a grading or measuring concept; it is a matter of relative standing on some criterion. It does not make sense to talk about people just "being equal," unless that is only a rhetorical way of expressing their common moral standing as human beings.[1] So when Allan, for example, writes about the "equal treatment of equal people," he must have in mind some criterion of equality for "treatment" and another for "people." Call these the *criteria of relevance*.

Settling on criteria of relevance requires a choice, for no two people are equal in all respects. In Allan's example, the two smokers may have the same habit, but different incomes; the two people with the same income might have different demands on it. Two people who were equal on every imaginable criterion (for example, in their wealth, income, education, weight, age, and location in space) would be the same person. Indeed, for any two different people there are infinitely many ways in which they are unequal. So when we enjoin policy makers to treat equal people equally with regard to taxation, we can really mean only this: treat equally those people who are equal in the relevant ways.

But what is relevant? There are two different approaches to determining this, and they give rise to two conceptions of equity, which I am going to call "interstitial equity" and "distributive equity."

Interstitial Equity

We might take as our criteria of relevance those provided by the existing policy itself, and look only for anomalies and inconsistencies within it. Brian Barry (1965, 153) has called this the "interstitial" use of equity: we criticize as inequitable deviations from principle, without regard to the possible justifications for the principle itself: "We merely have to take our stand on the principle that whatever is to be done should be done equally to all who are alike in what the rule itself declares to be the relevant respects." So, on the "interstitial" view of equity, all that is required is that a tax system treat people consistently and rationally.

This view is latent in the following passage: "The Carter Commission seems to have been confused between equity in the sense of fair and reasonable taxes *which is a matter pretty well confined to the tax system itself*, and equity in the sense of an equitable distribution of the national income, which is not limited to taxation but also includes government expenditures and government policies such as protection and regulation of industry and monetary policy" (Robinson 1967, 10; emphasis added). There are two points here: that overall social justice has to take into account both taxes and transfers, and that there is a sense of fair or equitable taxation that can be determined by just considering the tax system itself. If the latter means, as I think it must in this context, looking only to the rules themselves to determine the relevant similarities and differences among taxpayers, then it invokes the interstitial sense of equity.

Now, for some purposes, interstitial equity is a valuable concept. When we are considering the administration of justice, for example, we often appeal to a related standard (called "formal justice"). We do so because those who administer justice usually have little or no power unilaterally to change the rules they administer; their role involves applying the rules as given. There are several reasons for doubting that this is very helpful in formulating tax policy.

First, if one restricts oneself to questions of interstitial equity one fuses two properly independent questions: resource allocation and income distribution. As Barry (1965, 156) puts it: "If it is supposed that there is some 'equitable' way of sharing out any given tax burden, the main determinant of post-tax income distribution will be the *amount* of money raised in taxes, so that if (for example) the tax system is progressive those who seek greater equality of post-tax incomes will have to favour greater state expenditures and vice versa."

Second, it encourages policy makers to treat questions of substance as if they were questions of definition. For example, the Carter Report advocated that income tax be assessed on what it called the "discretionary income" of the taxpayer, which was in turn defined as consumption plus net change in savings for the taxable period, minus an amount necessary to maintain "the appropriate standard of living" for the taxpayer. But to derive progressive tax rates, it then defined the "appropriate" level of consumption as one that varies with income. As critics quickly realized, however, there is no way to derive or defend progressivity just on the basis of a certain definition of income.[2] Terms such as "income," "wealth," and "economic power" get defined only in the context of a more general theory about the nature and significance of the economic resources people ought to control. The substantive theory of justice has to come first.

Third, it is not even certain that interstitial equity is always desirable. Sometimes the wrong target is better missed.[3] Consider an unjust regulation: for instance, one requiring that the property of Japanese Canadians be uniformly expropriated. Suppose that an official takes pity on an especially poor Japanese family and, contrary to the order, exempts them from expropriation. This is a violation of interstitial equity. The rule requires like treatment of likes, and here there is, by hypothesis, no distinction recognized as relevant by the regulation. But for there to be any injustice, it seems reasonable to suppose that there must be someone who is wronged. Yet who is that? Not the exempted family, since by hypothesis the treatment that the rule mandated is itself unjust. What about the other Japanese families? Are they entitled to the even-handed application of an unjust rule? That hardly seems more likely. But if no one has been wronged, how can this violation of interstitial equity be unjust?

Finally, and most important, interstitial equity is a notion that can be applied only to an existing tax system. If one considers setting up a system *de novo* it tells us nothing to say that it is to be consistently administered. If one considers how an existing system might be reformed, it is not helpful to think in terms of interstitial equity either. Indeed, this is not really a goal of tax policy at all; it is a constraint on its other goals, requiring that they be pursued consistently.

For those reasons, interstitial equity is not very useful to the policy maker. Its prominence in the literature results, I suspect, from an inappropriate extension of the requirement of consistency in administering some policy to the very different context of formulating or defending a policy. Its overall effect is to distract attention from fundamental questions of distributive principle and to focus it, instead, on supposed problems of definition. That is why, to some, horizontal equity seems a more tractable notion than vertical equity; vertical equity makes explicit reference to evaluative judgements in its idea of "appropriately different" treatment. None the less, this is illusory, for the very criteria of relevant difference themselves make implicit appeal to those judgements. Moreover, when criteria of relevance are at issue, the distinction between vertical and horizontal equity becomes less important. Consider, for example, the position of two taxpayers, one of whom has an at-home spouse doing housework, whereas the other has to pay market rates for the same housekeeping services. When we try to evaluate their relative economic positions, are we studying a problem of horizontal or vertical equity? That will depend on the answer we give to the question of whether such housework ought to count among the resources that the taxpayer is held to control, and that will in turn depend on general considerations of distributive justice.

Distributive Equity

I am going to call conceptions of equity that incorporate independent criteria of relevance "distributive" to emphasize their relation to considerations of distributive justice. As the report of the Meade Committee (Institute for Fiscal Studies 1978, 12) rightly put it: "The final choice of redistributional aims for a tax system involves basic value judgements about the nature of a good society, which are matters for political decision." It is arguable that it is better to address these without invoking the term "equity" at all.[4] That may be right; its rhetorical attraction is that "equity" sounds less demanding than "justice" or "fairness." (Compare: "pay equity" and "a fair wage.") And the use of equity in this second, extended sense, is too entrenched to be easily dislodged.

From this viewpoint, the "relevant ways" in which people are equal depend on general considerations of distributive justice, not on the definition of terms. Consider, for example, the Carter Report's (1966, 14) recommendation of a broadening of the concept of income to provide a comprehensive tax base: "A dollar gained through the sale of a share, bond or piece of real property bestows exactly the same economic power as a dollar gained through employment or operating a business. The equity principles we hold dictate that both should be taxed in exactly the same way. To tax the gain on the disposal of property more lightly than other kinds of gains or not at all would be grossly unfair." The claim is that the source of economic power is not a relevant difference among individuals, though the quantity of it is. Whether this is a thesis we should endorse is not a matter of the "definition" of income; nor is it a problem of technical economic argument. It is not a thesis than can even be tested within the interstitial model of equity judgements. That it is "grossly unfair" to treat different sources of economic power differently can be only because to do so offends the animating principle of the report, that taxation should be based on ability to pay.

For all its vision and rigour, it is striking that so much of the argument of the Carter Report is packaged in the language of interstitial equity and so little is said in explicit defence of ability-to-pay principles. And the commission was not alone in this reticence. Even the federal New Democratic Party's 1987 report on personal income taxation said nothing to the point, apart from reference to the Carter Report on progressivity. One can understand the political reasons for avoiding substantive argument, particularly in an environment that is unfriendly to steeply progressive taxation. But this can wrongly encourage the view that there just is not much in the way of principled argument for progressivity.

Now, it is true that on its own no philosophical theory of distributive justice is going to spell out answers to questions about marginal tax rates, the appropriate base, and so on. That is because those answers turn on empirical questions (including, for example, the role of incentive effects and capital mobility) as well as matters of principle. But the principles are important none the less, for it is only by appealing to them that one can approach a firm justification for any tax policy. So we are inevitably driven back to the large questions of principle that we are so tempted to avoid. In the remainder of this paper, I want to canvass three theories of distributive justice in order to see what distributive equity might amount to. Though they represent a range of political opinion and method in moral theory, these are not the only possible theories, nor do I claim that any one of them should be endorsed without qualification. They are chosen solely for their level of theoretical development and their apparently persuasive power. What is so surprising, I think, is that they converge on the tacit principle underlying the Carter Report.

Libertarian Views

Libertarian philosophers take as their primary value the freedom to dispose of one's private property. That is one right-wing conception of what freedom amounts to. This view is normally thought to be, and is advertised as, an enemy of redistributive taxation and a friend of the unfettered market and minimal state. There are many strands of libertarian thought; here, I can explore only a few implications of one.

According to Robert Nozick (1974), the justice of any distribution of economic resources depends solely on how that distribution came about. Whether it is fair that some people languish in poverty while others live in luxury depends not on what life is really like for those people, or on what needs go unmet, but on how things got that way. If the poor took fair but foolish risks, for example, the rich need not now compensate them for it. If they lost out in a free market that put a low value on their resources, they need not be supported either, provided only that they do no worse under the market system than they would without one at all. By contrast, if the rich literally stole resources from the poor, or coerced them in the bargaining process, then the distribution would be unjust. It all depends on history.

That is the intuitive idea of libertarianism. As a theory, it has three parts. First, there is an account of justice in original acquisitions: before property can be traded on the market it has to be owned, so ownership is primary. Next, the theory specifies what counts as a just transfer of property: roughly speaking, uncoerced exchange, gifts, and bequests. In a perfect world, that would be the end of things. But in the real world, where injustice can arise in either acquisition or transfer, we also need a third part – the theory of just rectification.

It may seem that, on such a theory, redistribution cannot even arise in principle. Sometimes Nozick (1974, 149–50) himself writes that way. He says, for instance, that redistribution assumes that things are available for distribution, but in fact they are not, for everything is already someone's property.

Yet this is deceiving. Consider the first step. We need to ask what *form* property rights should take before we can tell whether redistributive taxation violates them. Nozick tries to answer a somewhat different question – *Which* allocation of absolute rights to exclusive property would be best? – and he concludes: one that allows no redistribution. But we should resist that very question. There are ways to allocate control over economic resources other than through absolute, exclusive rights. For example, our actual regime is a mixture of exclusive private-property rights, non-exclusive use rights, collective property rights, and so on. Nozick does not show that only a system of absolute, exclusive property rights is justifiable. If property comes with initial, built-in limitations, then one of the arguments against redistribution is blocked.

Nozick sometimes suggests that a regime of justice in acquisition as he envisages it is justified because it meets the following test: it leaves people no worse off than they otherwise would have been. Had there been no private property or free market but merely anarchy, things would be no better. Those who fare badly in the market – for instance, those with disabilities or few skills – would have been badly off anyway, so they have no ground in justice for complaint now. Clearly, that baseline of comparison is arbitrary and indefensible. We need to compare a libertarian scheme of ownership, not to anarchy, but to alternative, feasible systems of ownership, such as our own mix.

In any case, whatever the correct theory of property rights, it is certain that many things that most of us now own, including our incomes, were obtained through a series of transactions that, at least somewhere, had a tainted past. There has been just too much unfair expropriation, theft, and coercion throughout history for each to have a secure pedigree to his or her holdings. And, in a market system, that fact will affect the relative prices of everything. So some people are now undoubtedly poorer and others richer than they would be if there had been no injustice along the way.[5] There is, of course, no secure way of telling just who these people are, nor any accurate estimate of just how much they have wrongfully gained. But that is my point. A stringent form of libertarianism has to rest on an implausible view about the determinacy and inviolability of rights to private property. Whatever the truth about property holdings, they do not represent an untainted, neutral baseline. In the real world, therefore, the principle of justice in rectification will be important.

Perhaps, not surprisingly, this is the least developed part of Nozick's theory. Yet, conceding its importance, he draws a significant conclusion for our purposes: "These issues are very complex and are best left to a full treatment of the principle of rectification. In the absence of such a treatment applied to a particular society, one *cannot* use the analysis and theory presented here to condemn any particular scheme of transfer payments, unless it is clear that no considerations of rectification of injustice could apply to justify it" (231). But that is our actual position. It is certain that the history of our holdings is not fully just, and uncertain that progressive taxation is not a justifiable form of rectification in the circumstances. Notice that this is not a direct argument from libertarianism to redistribution. It is an indirect argument, showing that one apparently potent case against redistribution fails, and thus opens the door to an argument based on the view that progressive taxation is a reasonable second-best remedy to the ideal of exact rectification. In a realistic Nozickian view, redistributive taxation is justifiable in the real world as a rough system of reparative justice.

Utilitarianism

Despite its obvious affinities to the free-market model, libertarian theory is not in fact the most influential moral view among neoclassical economists. Here, some version of utilitarianism still holds sway. According to utilitarians, the fundamental goal of social policy is to maximize the total (or, sometimes, the average) amount of preference satisfaction in society. Things go well when people get what they want; they go best when that is maximized.

Often, a utilitarian framework is simply assumed without argument. In Musgrave's work (1987, 114), for instance, it is assumed that the fundamental value of justice is welfare maximization; that problems arise only from differing tastes and preferences, such as the choice between work and leisure: "Matters are simple if we are prepared to assume that people have similar tastes ... If this were the case, any tax, be it on peanuts or on income, would meet the test of equal treatment." Again, the Meade Report (1978, 14) thought that the grounding of tax principles on some notion of welfare needed no argument: "Any distributional principles involve some measurement of how well off a taxpayer is. But it is not always easy to determine what the relevant aspects of welfare for tax purposes are." Thus the debates are often about how to understand and measure welfare, and how best to maximize it. Little notice is taken of the intense criticism to which this general view has been subjected in contemporary ethical theory.[6]

Still, utilitarians are normally friendly to redistribution. From Edgeworth and Pigou down to contemporary writers, the belief in the diminishing marginal utility of economic resources has been one of the main supports for a redistributive scheme of taxation. Among philosophers, R.M. Hare (1992, 193–4) has been a consistent defender of utilitarianism. He says: "Diminishing marginal utility is the firmest support for policies of progressive taxation of the rich and other egalitarian measures." Of course, like all utilitarian arguments, this one is heavily dependent on the facts, and there are other consequences that compete, including the effect of disincentives and backlash from the well-off. But against those negative upshots of redistribution, Hare thinks we should also set the benefits that flow from satisfying the general desire for equality that results because "inequality itself has a tendency to produce envy, which is a disagreeable state of mind and leads people to do disagreeable things."

One of the difficulties (at least, in the opinion of its critics) is that utilitarianism is very vulnerable to factual assumptions. It recommends that we weigh the benefits of a redistributive scheme against all of its costs, and since all preferences count in principle, these costs include strategic bluffing that passes for incentive effects, ill-motivated backlash, and so on. Some theories of justice would refuse to give weight to such preferences, just as most would refuse to count the satisfaction of racist preferences as an argument against non-discrimination. In contrast, the utilitarian does not go behind tastes and preferences to ask whether they are themselves just; rather, justice is defined in terms of maximizing the satisfaction of any and all preferences.

Utilitarian theory can give, therefore, a contingent case for redistributive taxation of the ability-to-pay sort. But the case is sometimes plagued with indeterminacy. The classic papers on optimal-tax theory, for example, are very dependent on the factual assumptions made. Without apparent irony, J.A. Mirrlees (1971, 186) writes: "The optimum tax schedule depends upon the distribution of skills within the population, in such a complicated way that it is not possible to say in general whether marginal tax rates should be higher for high-income, low-income, or intermediate-income groups." Only under special assumptions does he derive his famous result that an optimal income tax is approximately linear with a negative tax for the worst off. But another rigorous treatment (Sheshinski 1971, 409), using the same model and some general assumptions about the individuals' utility functions, proves that "among all linear income-tax functions, the optimal tax is always progressive, i.e., it provides a positive lump-sum at zero income and has a positive marginal tax rate." So the general thrust of standard forms of utilitarianism is also favourable to redistributive taxation, though subject to certain factual assumptions.

Egalitarian Justice

The contingent character of the utilitarian case for redistribution has been noticed and criticized by many. H.C. Simon (1938, 14) voiced the worry, writing, "the case for equality (for less inequality) is enormously stronger than any utility foundation on which it can be rested." One contemporary, and very influential attempt to provide a non-utilitarian case for equality has been developed by John Rawls.

Rawls's general idea (1971, 303) is that "all social primary goods – liberty and opportunity, income and wealth, and the bases of self-respect – are to be distributed equally unless an unequal distribution of any or all of these goods is to the advantage of the least favoured." This general specification needs to be made more precise, for there may be conflicts. What should we do if an unequal distribution of liberty increases everyone's income? Or if an unequal distribution of income raises everyone's income but lessens the opportunity for advancement for those at the bottom? Rawls's reply (302) is to set up a priority system:

First principle – Each person is to have an equal right to the most extensive total system of equal basic liberties compatible with a similar system of liberty for all.

Second principle – Social and economic inequalities are to be arranged so that they are both:
   a) to the greatest benefit of the least advantaged, and
   b) attached to offices and positions open to all under conditions of fair equality of opportunity.

These principles are ranked in order: the first takes priority over the second (so that liberty can be restricted only for the sake of liberty, and not for economic advantages); the second takes priority over securing economic efficiency; and equality of opportunity itself takes priority over the "difference principle (2a)."

The priority rules mark this as a liberal kind of egalitarianism: one that prohibits restricting basic liberties (such as freedom of expression or association) even if to do so would make a society wealthier. And it is not the most stringent form of egalitarianism that we might imagine, for it does not rule out every inequality in income. It rules out only those inequalities that do not benefit the worst off. If a certain inequality does benefit them (say, by providing fair incentives to greater productivity), then it must be permitted, for to eliminate it would make the badly off even worse off.

Because of the limits on its egalitarianism, this is sometimes, wrongly, described as a "trickle-down" theory of justice, one that endorses any sort of disparities in economic resources provided that they result only in some sort of benefits for the badly off. Nothing could be farther from the truth. Rawls's theory does not permit an inequality merely on the ground that it has some, however slight, benefit to the poor. It requires the much more stringent condition that the inequality maximizes the position of the badly off. An equality that produces a slight benefit to the poor and enormous advantages to the well-off would be prohibited if a feasible arrangement without that inequality makes the poor even better off, notwithstanding that it comes at the expense of the enormous advantages to the well-off. Modest though it may seem to the radical egalitarian, the Rawlsian view is, in our circumstances, a fairly demanding one.

Rawls's argument for these principles is complex and controversial. It has two thrusts. First, it appeals to our intuitive notion that it is unfair for individuals to be disadvantaged by social circumstances or natural talents for which they are not responsible. Second, Rawls thinks that these principles are such that people who were deciding in advance about the rules of justice to govern their society would agree to them if they wanted to do well for themselves but did not know where they would end up on the social ladder. The difference principle, in particular, may be seen as a kind of insurance against ending up at the bottom, for it guarantees that the bottom is as high as it can be.

This gives a more direct and robust justification of redistributive taxation than do the other theories considered here. In the libertarian view, redistribution is permissible as a matter of rectification; for the utilitarian, it is a means to maximizing the general welfare; but for the liberal egalitarian, it is a direct requirement of justice itself.

It is not possible to scrutinize these principles further here, nor is doing so necessary for our present purposes. For we have seen enough to establish one, perhaps surprising, conclusion. I began by noticing that such terms as "equity," "fairness," and "justice" are essentially contested concepts subject to deep disagreement about values. Although we have found no reason to revise that view, it is also interesting that prominent theories from the right to the left of the political spectrum can all give principled reasons for endorsing a system of redistributive taxation. As accounts of distributive equity, they provide what was missing from the interstitial approach. They suggest that policy makers who endorse an ability-to-pay approach to taxation should be able to communicate to the public plausible justifications for the policy rather than providing them with arbitrary definitions. On a variety of grounds, it can be argued that fairly sharing the burden of the state is a matter of justice and not socially organized charity.

Conclusion

Fair taxation, I have suggested, is a tax regime that is substantively just. This cannot be understood through the "interstitial" model of equity, according to which tax fairness is about consistent treatment of likes, and appropriately different treatment of unlikes. We need criteria of relevance that can be derived only from principles of distributive justice. The power of the interstitial model is great, however, and often leads policy makers to try to reason as if they were adjudicators, attempting fairly to apply rules someone else had laid down. But when one's task is to lay down or reform the rules themselves, this cannot work.

What is needed is an open and direct assessment of the justice of redistribution. This is a difficult and value-charged matter, and there are competing theories. But I think it significant that influential contemporary theories of justice, whether of the right, centre, or left, endorse significant redistribution of economic resources. Indeed, I think it very likely, though I will not argue the point here, that they all endorse more redistribution than our tax system actually provides. It is true that they differ in nature and in rationale. But there is a quite astonishing degree of practical consensus from what are otherwise competing, abstract theories.

Notes

The first draft of this paper was prepared for the Ontario Fair Tax Commission and completed in February 1992. I have profited from the comments of Allan Maslove and Leo Panitch on an earlier draft of this paper.

1 See, for example, Williams (1962) and Vlastos (1984).
2 Cf. McIntyre (1988).
3 See Lyons (1973).
4 Westen (1982) has criticized certain notions of "equality" in law along these lines. Cf. Barry (1965, 152): "The principle of equity is that equals should be treated equally, and unequals unequally. If the principle is taken to include within itself criteria for determining what makes people "equal" and what makes them "unequal," then it swallows all other comparative distributive principles."
5 See Lyons (1981).
6 See, especially, Smart and Williams (1973).

Bibliography

Allan, C.M. 1971. *The Theory of Taxation.* Harmondsworth: Penguin

Barry, B. 1965. *Political Argument.* London: Routledge and Kegan Paul

Canada. Royal Commission on Taxation. 1966. Report (Carter Report), Vol. 1. Ottawa: Queen's Printer

Carter Report. *See* Canada, Royal Commission on Taxation

Connolly, William E. 1974. *The Terms of Political Discourse,* 2d ed. Lexington, MA: Heath

Hare, R.M. 1992. "Justice and Equality." In *Justice: Alternative Political Perspectives,* 2d ed., ed. J.P. Sterba, 105–19. Belmont, CA: Wadsworth

Institute for Fiscal Studies. 1978. *The Structure and Reform of Direct Taxation: Report of a Committee Chaired by Prof. J.E. Meade* (Meade Report). London: Allen and Unwin

Lyons, David. 1973. "On Formal Justice." *Cornell Law Review,* 58: 833–61

– 1981. "The New Indian Claims and Original Rights to Land." In *Reading Nozick,* ed. J. Paul, 355–79. Oxford: Blackwell

McIntyre, M.J. 1988. "What Should Be Redistributed in a Redistributive Income Tax? Retrospective Comments on the Carter Commission Report." In *The Quest for Tax Reform: The Royal Commission on Taxation Twenty Years Later,* ed. N. Brooks, 189–209. Toronto: Carswell

Meade Report. *See* Institute for Fiscal Studies

Mirrlees, J.A. 1971. "An Exploration in the Theory of Optimum Income

Taxation." *Review of Economic Studies*, 38: 175–208

Musgrave, R.A. 1959. *The Theory of Public Finance*. New York: McGraw-Hill

— 1987. "Equity Principles in Public Finance." In *The Relevance of Public Finance for Policy-Making*, ed. H.M. van de Kar, 113–23. Detroit: Wayne State University Press

New Democratic Party/Tax Probe. 1987. *The Personal Income Tax System: In Search of Fairness*. Ottawa: Tax Probe

Nozick, R. 1974. *Anarchy, State and Utopia*. New York: Basic Books

Pigou, A. 1928. *A Study in Public Finance*. London: Macmillan

Rawls, J. 1971. *A Theory of Justice*. Cambridge, MA: Harvard University Press

Robinson, A.J. 1967. "The Concept of Equity in the Carter Report." In *Canada's Tax Structure and Economic Goals*, ed. A.J. Robinson and J. Cutt, 1–13. Downsview, ON: York University Faculty of Administrative Studies

Sheshinski, E. 1971. "The Optimal Linear Income-Tax." In *Economic Justice: Selected Readings*, ed. E.S. Phelps, 409–16. Harmondsworth: Penguin

Simons, H.C. 1938. *Personal Income Taxation*. Chicago: University of Chicago Press

Smart, J.C.C., and B. Williams. 1973. *Utilitarianism: For and Against*. Cambridge: Cambridge University Press

Vlastos, G. 1984. "Justice and Equality." In *Theories of Rights*, ed. J. Waldron, 41–76. Oxford: Oxford University Press

Westen, Peter. 1982. "The Empty Idea of Equality." *Harvard Law Review*, 75: 537–96

Williams, B. 1962. "The Idea of Equality." In *Philosophy, Politics and Society*, 2d ser., ed. P. Laslett and W.G. Runciman, 110–31. Oxford: Blackwell

4 Equitable and Fair
Widening the Circle[1]

A. MARGUERITE CASSIN

This paper explores how to think about fairness in relation to taxation. It seeks to make a paradigm shift, moving away from assuming the rationality and neutrality of the disciplines involved in creating the theory and practice of tax. Instead it argues for investigating tax practices and associated discourse as a social organization. I use feminist method and scholarship to problematize rationality and neutrality and argue that we need to seek fairness in relation to the everyday realities of people's lives.

Tax: The Technical Is Political

As an everyday matter tax is viewed as political, inevitable, and a matter beyond the control of ordinary people. Rather than accept this observation as self-explanatory, I want to explore how tax is, at the same time, both political – that is, within the domain of social action – and objectified – that is, beyond the control of everyday life. In this section of the paper I explore two ways of seeing tax as political. First, I review the argument offered by Murray Dobbin as an example of how tax is analysed as a site of political struggle in which individuals and groups forward their interests. Second, I introduce a discussion of how the technical and professional practices of creating tax are also a matter of social practice.

In certain contexts, tax is understood as a political matter. Murray Dobbin, in a program for CBC "Ideas" titled "Tax: The Second Certainty" (April 1992), makes explicit the political and power-based character of taxation.[2] He documents the opposition of wealthy in-

dividuals and business corporations to progressive or fair-tax reform
in the cases of the Carter Commission and the Benson and Mac-
Eachern budgets. This opposition has included capital and investment
strikes. The major consequence of these forms of political opposition
has been that tax changes are now proposed publicly only after they
have been vetted and given support by the tax community. Dobbin
and others point out that the tax community is largely composed of
lawyers, accountants, and economists whose practices and positions
are founded in work for wealthy individuals and business corporations. This situates the technical professional domain of tax within a
circle of influence in which professionals who earn their living by
representing wealthy individuals and business corporations vet and
sanction tax changes.

As it turns out, when the tax community calls for tax reform, which
it has done for more than two decades in Canada, it is not asking for
more progressive taxation, which would take the form of closing loopholes, abandoning regressive tax incentives, and focusing tax on personal and corporate income. Dobbin argues that this is true in spite
of a general acknowledgement that it has been evident for three decades that the unfairness of the tax system is one of the most pressing
issues affecting economic activity. Instead, the tax community (and
the business community, led by the Business Council on National
Issues) supports and has been lobbying for reform that creates a "level
playing-field" for business in relation to the United States. This tax
reform, Dobbin argues, which is now well under way with the Mulroney government, involves increasing the rate and magnitude of the
shift of the tax burden onto middle- and low-income Canadians, reducing tax on wealthy individuals and creating a tax climate that
supports and enhances free trade with the United States. The overall
consequence is that capital becomes more mobile and less accessible
to existing forms of taxation.

Dobbin argues that the politics of taxation in Canada is organized
to favour wealthy individuals and business corporations who, essentially, have shown themselves unwilling to pay taxes and who have
the power to set the agenda in terms of tax. This, Dobbin argues, is
the basis of the unfairness of the tax system. Panitch broadens this
view as he explores the general nature of the politics of taxation in
his paper in this volume. He begins by recognizing that unfair taxes
have persisted transnationally in the face of knowledge, ideology,
and government commitment.

These discussions of tax and economic and social interests are important. They demonstrate that tax issues are vital to all citizens. However, beyond objecting to the amount of tax they pay, it appears that ordinary citizens have little to say about tax questions and are powerless and often inactive in the face of tax changes.[3] In this context, tax appears to be a matter of fact, entirely self-evident. So we come to an interesting disjuncture. On the one hand, tax is obviously political and a matter subject to competing interests; on the other hand, it seems that tax is a self-evident factual matter that is difficult to debate.

How can these two "hands" be part of the same social world? How can tax be both political and "factual" at the same time? I believe that investigating this question leads us to examine the social practices that create the factual properties of tax. These are the creation of the professional and technical organization of tax, the foundations for which are found within the disciplines of accounting, law, and economics.

Law, accounting, and economics in the area of tax are concerned with two basic questions: Who will pay? How and on what basis will they pay? These are matters which within these disciplines are seen as separate from politics. In her outstanding study of women and tax, Kathleen Lahey (1988b, i) cites a tax specialist who commented on his own experience of receiving his training in tax: "I could not understand how people could ignore the politics of the tax system. It was difficult for me to sit through my classes knowing that off campus, people were eating garbage." The account identifies a key dimension of how tax is constructed as a specialization and as a practice. Tax is separated from politics and power, and ultimately from people, by creating the study and practice of tax as a technical activity, engaged in largely by accountants, lawyers, and economists.

We are habituated to technical practices both as forms of knowledge and as modes of organization in our society (Hacker 1990; Franklin 1991; Smith 1990a; Cassin 1990). Technical matters are exhibited as science, technology, and management/administration. Technical matters appear to be factual and commonsensical, and at the same time require highly specialized knowledge to create, explain, and design. Technical matters may use commonsense language, but at the same time the lexicon is technical and specialized.

Tax is technical in keeping with the general pattern. It is a legal, professional, and administrative matter that is the purview of accountants, lawyers, and economists. Our forms of tax rely upon monetary social organization, that is, upon organizing relationships among people through quantitative and ultimately money-based equivalence. The objects of tax are wealth, income, and consumption. Tax is primarily thought about in terms of units of taxation, quantity, and effects on economic activity.

The technical character of tax makes people disappear; they are not present in the institutional domain of tax. The messiness of people's lives and interests do not exist within tax in its technical form. The realities of everyday/night life appear as idiosyncratic in the face of tax technology. Instead tax is "grounded" by behavioural assumptions about people, formulated primarily within economics. Ordinary citizens can participate in discussion only on the grounds established through tax categories; any other basis seems externalized – off the wall.

Feminist scholarship has problematized and investigated this separation between everyday life and the forms of institutional organization. Women have faced inequality in their everyday lives, and at the same time it has seemed that this had nothing to do with the public world of politics, economy, and civil society. Feminist scholarship has developed methods with which to investigate the technical, professional, managerial, legal, and rational practices through which our society is ruled.

Beginning from women's silence, demoralization, and low self-esteem; our absence (as women) from politics, professions, business, art, literature, and the sites where knowledge is created; our containment in "female" occupations and professions; the lack of recognition for women's non-waged contributions to family and public life; and the psychological, psychiatric, medical, philosophical, and political characterizations of women as separate from and intellectually and rationally inadequate in comparison with men, feminist scholars have discovered, formulated, and analysed women's social inequality. This scholarship has offered a contribution to social action.

These discoveries about the relation of everyday realities and the associated research epistemology and method help us understand the properties of contemporary institutional organization. These discoveries suggest that both the absence of people within the categories and constructs of tax and the professional ground as the basis for the discussion of tax are political expressions of how tax is organized. There is an intimate connection between tax and people eating garbage. However, this connection is expressed politically in a separation between tax and poverty.

Women and Tax: The Everyday World as Problematic[4]

In this section, I show how feminist methods and discoveries are being used to investigate the relation of women and tax and to illuminate tax practices themselves. The purpose of the discussion is methodological. It is not intended to review all the arguments and discussions about women and tax. Rather, it shows how feminists have worked from everyday experience to raise questions about apparently neutral scholarly concepts and institutional practices.

Women are poor and dependent. The work women do for pay earns them only a portion of what men earn for the work they do for pay. Much of the work women do is not paid. Women's work does not give them access to holding positions of authority and power in our society. Women do not create the knowledge that is used to organize and govern our society. These are everyday realities for women. Given women's circumstance in the economy, one might expect that women would pay less tax than men and have more services available through government expenditures.

Lahey (1988b) conducted a review of the 1985 tax year in which she assembles a review of the facts. She summarizes the tax situation for women: "Women in Canada are overtaxed, relative to men. There are several ways to express this over taxation. One way is to express all taxes paid by women and men as a percentage of their shares of money incomes: on this measure, women pay 45.6 percent of their incomes as taxes, while men pay only 30 percent. Another way is to calculate women's and men's shares of all after tax incomes: even though they started out with only 32 percent of all incomes, women receive only 26.8 percent of all after tax money incomes, while men's share is 73.2 percent (2–3; cf. tables on 195, 198, and 200).[5]

Feminists are showing that tax is a problem for women. Using discoveries from feminist method and analysis, scholars have approached tax in relation to women's realities. We are seeing the formulation of a three-dimensional examination: a gathering of facts[6] about women and tax, an investigation of the concepts and practices of tax in view of the everyday realities of women's lives, and a consideration of how the facts represent and are part of the concepts and practices that concert and order social relations among men and women.

A preliminary examination of the orthodox tax literature displays an absence of consideration of the topic in relation to women. This absence is an expression of how both the literature and tax practices themselves are put together. Feminists began considering the relation of women to tax in Canada under the Royal Commission on the Status of Women (1970) through a report that used an orthodox framework.

Since then, women's organizations have brought a number of tax issues forward for consideration. In various ways, the issues raised by women have tried to introduce the realities of women's lives into tax theories and practices. They have focused on issues of children, marital relations, and family. This focus is the consequence of both the importance of these relationships to women and the issues created by the tax system itself. Lahey (1988a, 6) points out that "A number of specific provisions of the Income Tax Act apply such blatantly sexist stereotypes or have such obviously disparate impact on women that they can be considered to discriminate against women. These are the structure of the spousal credit, the transferable credits for dependent spouses, the alimony and child support provisions and the provisions relating to children, including the childcare expense deduction."

A key issue in feminist scholarship has been the discovery that women are uniformly absent as the subject of scholarly investigation.[7] This absence can be attributed, presumably, to the assumption that investigation of the species has included women. As research has variously tried to include women, a "peculiar eclipsing"[8] has been encountered; women and their realities disappear in the face of general theoretical frameworks, methodological practices, and orthodoxies of objectivity in the disciplines. Further investigation has led to the discovery that men, in making the scholarly disciplines, have taken up their interests, realities, and social location. Men have situated themselves in and occupy the general, the neutral, objective ground (of science).

The implication of men's dominance over scientific topic and investigation is that women are silenced by scientific objectivity. The knowledge of science/social science central to the creation of our social order is and has been created by and for men. Where women have participated, it has been within the strict boundaries of the orthodoxies of topic and tenets of objectivity. These discoveries about orthodox science and social science have opened the epistemological horizons, methods of investigation, and foundation of objectivity itself to investigation. In this way, objectivity has become a subject for investigation in feminist scholarship.[9] The result has been the beginning of the making of feminist method, pedagogy, epistemology, ontology, and knowledge in its own right in relation to many disciplines.

The tax practices identified by Lahey have been and are being challenged by the picture of women's inequality that has been built up through feminist scholarship on the family. Sociology and anthropology have been leading disciplines in which family has been researched and theorized. The central tenet of orthodox sociological thinking has been the assumption of a nuclear, hierarchical, patriarchal family as the universal form of family at the core of civilized society (Goode 1982; Hale 1990). This view of the family is made from the position of the male head of household and contemporary patriarchy. It is ahistorical and has always stood in opposition to empirical anthropological findings. Nevertheless, this view has anchored assumptions about procreation, socialization, residence patterns, and the economic order of families (Hale 1990) and has heavily influenced social policy. Examination of tax practices in relation to the family reveals that just such assumptions about the family are at the heart of income tax provisions (Lahey 1988b).

Feminist sociology has addressed itself to the character and practical and social organization of family. In particular, Margrit Eichler (1988) has shown the orthodoxy of family sociology to have no empirical ground in the everyday organization and conduct of families. On the basis of an ongoing examination of family organization, she critiques the dominant sociological paradigm and creates a study of the social organization of families. She has identified and described the various arrangements in which families are constituted. Eichler's work shows that nuclear family–based assumptions of residence, socialization, and economic cooperation do not empirically specify and therefore do not adequately generalize contemporary Canadian families.

By examining the situation of children, men, and women, Eichler has made an important contribution that has the capacity both to critique existing policy and programs and to offer direction for revision in social, economic, and tax policy and practices. When the tax practices of the transferable credits of dependent spouses; alimony and child-support provisions; and the provisions relating to children, including the child care–expense deduction are examined in light of the realities of family organization provided by Eichler's work, we can see that these practices do not address the realities of the lives of men, women, and children.[10] Instead, tax categories, which create the "terrain for tax," begin in male-based assumptions about the structure of the family, the power relations in families, and the character of family organization and men's need for protection from "gold-bricking" wives.[11] The tax categories create an apparently neutral domain since they apply the same criteria to all families. At the same time, the tax practices created intensify the inequality of women and the privilege of men, which is already structured by low pay, sex segregation in the labour force, and household and child work.

The problems in the tax system for women should not be seen to be confined to salaried income. Beth Symes has brought an action in response to the denial of allowance of the expenses of a nanny for her children as a tax-deductible business expense by Revenue Canada.[12] The case makes use of scholarship on women and entrepreneurship, which finds that women are starting their own businesses to seek independence, advancement, and recognition, and to accommodate work and family responsibilities.[13] It is obvious to women that they cannot undertake demanding careers (with long and unpredictable hours) and have children, without the work of additional people (normally women) and institutions (child-care facilities). In view of what counts as business expenses, the denial of these expenses seems anomalous. It also offers insight into the assumptions that underpin the allowance of business expenses.[14]

The discussions of tax in the feminist movement and in feminist scholarship have opened important debates on issues of women and tax. For example, there is a debate about whether a child care–expense deduction is the proper mode in which to provide for the care of children whose parents work in the labour force. Many feminist organizations advocate a publicly funded national child-care program that would ensure adequate care for children from all economic and social backgrounds and would be paid for by all Canadians. Questions are being raised about the propriety of the tax arrangements for child support, which treat the funds as income to the adult – normally a woman – in receipt of the payments. An alternative view suggests that this offers an income-splitting benefit to separated or divorced couples.

Important advances in the critique of tax policy in relation to women have been made by presenting the everyday family lives of women as the basis of a critique of tax policy. These considerations of women and tax are characterized by the way in which they note defects in or problems for women in tax policy and propose alterations in tax practices. At the same time, they offer a window into the social assumptions that underlie the tax practices.

Kathleen Lahey (1988b) has begun the process of making a systematic critique of tax that incorporates the thinking in the emerging body of feminist scholarship on work, family, law, and political economy. She offers a remarkable examination of women and tax in a study that develops a "feminist approach to tax law and economic policy" (1988b, 1). Her study offers an examination of women and tax that takes into consideration both feminist theory and analysis, and economic, social, and tax policy and practices. It explores women and tax in relation to poverty, work, tax types, and tax reform. Lahey (1988b, iv) reflects upon how she began her work and the first considerations: "Like most women who specialize in income taxation, I first became interested in the topic while thinking about the grand sweeping tax policy controversies of this century, such as the proper definition of the tax base (should housewives' "imputed income" be included in their taxable income?), the tax unit (should husbands and wives be treated as a marital unit or as individuals?), the rate structure (are the inequities that result from a progressive rate structure which is riddled with exemptions and deductions justified?)." As she explored tax, she began to consider it in relation to her own experience and the general condition of women. This offered her insight into orthodox analysis of tax policy and women: "I ... realized that when tax policy analysts focus their inquiries on 'goldbricking' wives and the economic advantages of cohabitation for women, they are not talking about the world that most women live in" (ibid). Her work is situated quite differently: "it is out of the struggle to explain why women who live in Toronto might ever have to think about eating garbage – let alone actually do it – that I have approached this project in the way I have: an approach that is grounded in the realities of women's poverty and dispossession, articulated as a critique of both political economy and income tax theory, and aimed at integrating women's concerns into the income tax policy formation process" (iii).

As feminist scholars in sociology and anthropology have explored their disciplines, the relation of women's poverty to paid work has been uncovered. Orthodox sociological conceptions of work have been rooted in male relations to paid work. Until recently, therefore, work has been studied as paid work. As long as this orthodoxy was maintained, the family was treated as an institution of socialization, and gender was not seen as relevant to work.

From the social location of women, work is a continuum from paid work in the economy to unpaid work undertaken for children and husbands. The phenomenon of women working both in the labour force and in the home has been formulated as a double day of labour (Benston 1974). This brings the family into view as a workplace for women. The work involves an extended work organization of physical, emotional, psychological, spiritual, and managerial work (Luxton

1980; Oakley 1974; Smith 1987). Moreover, the restricted locations of women in paid work and the minimized value of their work are illuminated by examining the relation of house-based work and paid work (Armstrong 1974; Armstrong and Armstrong 1984). So we can see a pattern of inequality organized in relation to the valuation of the labour of love women do in families and the oppression displayed by their situation in the labour force.

The observation of women's work as being both paid and unpaid offers a window into the conception and social organization of the economy. The work women do for their families, while unpaid, is relied upon by both men and children. Women's work in the home is relied upon by the school (Manicom 1988; Griffith 1984; Griffith and Smith 1985, Smith 1987), and, more generally, the practices of child-rearing are relied upon to socialize a new generation of workers (Burstyn and Smith 1985). For men, women's work in the home and in personal relationships provides the base from which they do paid work. When this line of thinking is pursued, it becomes clear that employers, and indeed the relations of capital itself, rely upon the work of women as a basis for the conduct of commercial relations.

The unpaid work of women should not be seen to be confined to domesticity. Waring (1988) documents the wide array of work women do (in growing food and making goods) that is unacknowledged in national income accounting but, provides real and necessary contributions to the lives of their husbands, children, and countries. We might test this by asking: If women's unpaid work did not exist, would the economy – indeed, the species – exist? The answer is, of course, they would not. These observations bring us to the inescapable conclusion that the "market" economy depends upon unpaid work of women; moreover, women's unpaid work is appropriated to the economy, and ultimately to men.

Lahey recognizes that our existing economic organization presupposes men's appropriation of women's unpaid labour. She shows that the tax system contributes to, supports, and enforces this appropriation of women's paid labour to men (1988b, 3):

The difference in women's shares of pretax and aftertax incomes is due to the impact of the total tax structure. This measure shows that while the total tax structure adds to women's poverty, it actually increases men's total share of incomes. On a third measure, women are overtaxed by 20 percent in the indirect tax system (sales, property, gasoline and excise taxes) and by 4 percent in the income tax system. Although the

income tax structure is said to moderate the admittedly regressive incidence of indirect taxation, both systems actually tax women regres-
sively and both systems add to the overtaxation of women.

She goes on to illustrate the way in which women come to pay 52
per cent of all indirect taxes and are overtaxed, as compared with
men, within the income categories of the income tax. Moreover, Lahey
contends that "recent tax reforms intensify the overtaxation and regressive taxation of women" (5–7).

The organization of tax supports and enhances a property relation
in which men own and dispose of the vast majority of property (Lahey
1988b, 45–52). In a society where social will is embedded in property,
this issue is critical. Lahey raises questions about the assumptions of
family and individual on which tax practices are based, and on which
new proposals are being developed (53–71). She reviews and recon-
siders critiques of tax-policy analysis: "Women's critiques of main-
stream tax policy analysis have challenged it on three levels: the
assumptions that shape the conceptual terrain of tax policy analysis;
the ways those assumptions have affected 'scientific' inquiries into
the effects of taxation; the importance that is attached to women and
women's concerns in the policy formation process" (1988b, 289). Here
we see that the conceptions of both tax and the social organization
being taxed are askew in relation to the realities of women's lives.
Tax reform has been based upon both poor analysis and inadequate
grasp of the relation of tax and everyday realities.

What, then, can we make of these considerations of tax and wom-
en's everyday realities? The conceptions of tax are not neutral for
women. Women's inequality is visible in relation to access to jobs
and the pay they receive for the work they do in the economy. This
inequality is intensified when the disproportionate financial and
unpaid-work responsibility women bear in relation to household and
children is considered. Tax policies take into consideration the social
world from the location of men. As such, tax is part of constructing
the patriarchal relations of inequality.

Women, Tax, and the Regime of Rationality

The focus on wealth, income, and consumption as the objects for tax
theory and practice appears to create a neutral domain, external to
people and therefore to the inequalities of gender, race, class and
disability, environmental considerations, and other lived realities. Tax

theory and its objects are the product of rational theorizing that situates tax within the domain of science and rational administration
rather than within the domain of speculation or subjectivity. In this
section I review the current feminist discussions of rationality and
neutrality. These discussions investigate both rationality and neutrality as a social construction. The point of the section is to introduce
the idea that rational constructs are gendered and have had a part in
subordinating women to men in society. This idea raises the need for
the investigation of social-organization tax theory and practices. This
discussion does not suggest that there cannot be rational constructs
that promote equality. It simply points out that existing practices have
been found to be part of creating women's inequality.

Seen as a social organization, rationality has been a central construct
in ordering and forming our knowledge, including, of course, the
formulations on which tax policy is based. As feminist scholarship
has shown us, women have been excluded from participating in creating rational knowledge. Our silence as women is a consequence of
this exclusion.

At the most general level, feminist scholars have addressed wom-
en's externalization from making knowledge and the bifurcated at-
tribution of characteristics to men and women so that women seem
unsuited to and incapable of sustained participation in the creation
of intellectual work (Smith 1992). Women and things feminine are
seen to threaten rational knowledge itself (Hacker 1990). Feminists
have examined the making of knowledge and, in particular, the making of science/social science. Women's absence from making knowledge has many dimensions. Historical work has shown that women
have created and contributed to the creation of knowledge, and these
contributions have been appropriated by and attributed to men (Harding 1986; Keller 1985; Smith 1987, 1990b). We have also learned that
women's "traditional" knowledge has been actively repressed. When
women have attempted to participate in the creation of rational/
scientific knowledge, they have been subject to an extended practice
of externalization and marginalization that continues in the present
(Harding 1986; Keller 1985; Smith 1987, 1990b).

Women's exclusion and silence have been explored in relation to
the foundational precepts – the individual, equality, and community
– that underpin the state, civil society, and the rule of law in our
society, as theorized by the British empiricists. Investigations by feminist legal scholars have shown that women were not included in this
historical conception of the individual (MacKinnon 1987; Lahey 1987,

1988b). Moreover, the individual (man) envisaged by Hobbes, Locke, Kant et al. was a man of *commerce* – if you will, a commercial man. In practical terms, the rule of law and the accompanying body of legal precedent have been created without consideration for or knowledge of the circumstances of women. In this respect, it stands as partial.

The universality and inclusiveness characteristic of the liberal democratic state have been fashioned on the basis of men's experience and knowledge of themselves, women, and the social and physical world. This universality and inclusiveness of law and the state are created by and for men, but of course women are and have been subject to it. Lahey (1988b, 3–4) formulates the consequences of these conceptions and the project of women's legal theory: "Law cannot be said to be the sole cause of women's disadvantaged status. Nonetheless, laws and legal processes operate powerfully to define the terms of women's oppression and therefore to form part of the material base of that oppression. A feminist theory of women and the law is thus about the ways in which law reflects and reinforces the social economic and political structures that surround subject women in patriarchal cultures."

The existence of man-made law has broad consequences. Mary Eberts (1986, 1991) has discussed how, in her legal practice, she discovered that facts about women's lives are not warrantable, and therefore not easily entered into legal evidence. She points to how this problem of acceptable evidence displays the practice of the exclusion of women's realities from the body of law, and, at the same time, opens a strategy for change. Feminist lawyers and legal theorists have been using the work of feminist scholars from other fields and their own research and legal practice to discover and introduce women's realities to legal theory and the courts (cf. Berger 1980; Boyle and Noonan 1986; Eberts 1985a, 1985b; Gallighar 1987; Gavigan 1986; Mossman 1986; O'Brien and McIntyre 1986; Sheehy 1987; Symes 1987).[15]

The most systematic effort to bring women's realities before the courts and into the body of law has been undertaken by the Women's Legal Education and Action Fund (LEAF). Razack (1990) has characterized LEAF as working with the rights framework to introduce a wide range of issues of women's inequality with the hope of opening up and broadening legal concepts themselves. The point is to create and expand legal concepts that take into account the realities of men's and women's lives and that can consider the inequality of women, and, in contrast, the relative privilege of men.[16] The interpretation and definition of equality are the focus of LEAF's work.[17]

The interrogation of women's silence and exclusion has opened a feminist critique of law and legal practice. It has begun the creation of a feminist jurisprudence and body of legal knowledge that seek to "widen the circle" of legal concepts to include the realities of women's lives. Similar developments are taking place in other disciplines and sites where knowledge is made in our society, as feminists explore the realities of women's lives. As this is developed, we can question the sex-typing of forms of social behaviour and therefore the forms of exclusion on the basis of it.

Dorothy Smith (1992), in an important breakthrough, takes up the issue of sex-bifurcated characterizations in relation to rationality and ruling. She observes: "Ascribing characteristic types of behaviour to one sex or the other is the effect of a regime and not of nature" (211). In interrogating this issue, she offers a companion line of analysis in the discussion of women's exclusion from the creation of knowledge. Smith examines women's exclusion as an active social process that is the product of ordering men's and women's relations through the regime of rationality: "The notion of a regime is that of an order imposed and regulated. Using the notion of a regime of rationality takes us beyond rationality as a mode of thinking and discourse or as a paradigm for ordering the relation of thought and action. The regime of rationality shifts attention from rationality as ideas, concepts, methods in general to rationality as a social order, as social organization concerting the activities of actual individuals. And hence among other matters as ordering relations among men and women" (208).

She argues that women's exclusion from making knowledge, through the regime of rationality, has, at its base, irrationality. Rather than working to admit men and women to the realm of ideas on the basis of logic, it secures the privilege of masculinity and the subordination of femininity.

If we see rationality as an active process of ordering relations between men and women, we can then see how to examine further the technical practices involved in tax. In this respect, tax is a regime in the same sense that rationality is. To paraphrase Smith: tax is a social order; a social organization concerting the activities of actual individuals. It orders, among other things, the relations among men and women. An examination of tax as a regime would yield an analysis of how it orders such relations, with the resulting tax effects described by Lahey.

The briefest examination of the accounting and economics literature displays that gender relations are assumed. Indeed, tax is focused upon ordering (legal) individuals within and in relation to commercial/economic relations. The rational technical categories of wealth, income, and consumption define the domain of tax. These locate the issues of concern in tax research, conceptualization, and organization.

In seeing tax as a regime for ordering the relations of individuals in view of commercial/economic relations, it becomes clear that social considerations are taken up within this context and not as matters with their own integrity. This situation is displayed by taking up everyday matters and exploring them in relation to tax. Everyday realities, in all their particularities, appear anomalous in the context of tax; they appear to introduce irrational externalities.

As we raise questions about tax from the everyday realities of women and from the analysis of inequality, we can see that gender relations are critical in tax policy, and more generally in our social order. Women's inequality both depends upon and is organized in the regime of tax. Moreover, by opening up tax to these questions we raise more than gender issues. We raise the issue of the reality the regime of tax is part of constructing and organizing, and dependent upon. The answer lies, in part, in an examination of how power and authority are organized and practised in society.

We learn from feminist analysis to examine foundational institutional principles from the realities of women's lives. We discover that the knowledge we have of our social and physical world has been developed and organized by and for men and is constituted as the domain of the objective, general, and neutral. Finally, the relations among individuals are expressed in ideas. We can then examine disciplines not only for their concepts and methods, but for how their ideas are active in creating the existing social order. In this respect, rationality can be seen to be a regime and can be examined to determine how it is used to organize relations between men and women. Tax, embedded as it is in the technical domain of rationality, can be examined to determine how it orders relations among people.

Conceptual Practices of Power[18]

In this section, I introduce a discussion of how the neutrality and rationality of tax is organized practically and empirically. I point to how practices of textual communication are organized to construct a reality that forms the basis for administration. This reality is the basis for the exercise of power.

The technical character of tax is a barrier to empirical investigation of the contribution of the tax discourse to the relation of tax, politics, and power when it is treated as neutral and factual. In our society, we have generally embedded technical practices into bureaucratic and organizational forms. The institutional and organizational ground for tax laid down by legal, economic, and accounting discourse is embedded in rationality, logic, and routine managerial practices. These create a seamless technical practice – a tax technology.[19] The notion of a tax technology formulates the way tax is conducted in an administrative terrain. The topics of tax are transpersonal and extralocal. They are not formed in or held by the contexts of the local, particular places in which we live out our lives, although, of course, they reach into and order those realities. Tax and tax administration appear to be equally applied and neutrally conceived. This conception is equated with political and social neutrality and equality. These aspects of organization are constructed in particular ways.

From an initial examination of women and tax we encounter an anomaly. From the social location of women, tax contributes to women's inequality. At the same time, tax is authoritatively conceptualized, constructed, ordered, and administered as neutral and uniform. How can these matters be true at the same time?

The regime of tax operates to organize relations among people through the routine practices in which power is organized in our society. Power is organized through concepts that stand as reality (Smith 1990b). We can see this clearly in the previous discussion of feminist explorations of the concepts of the individual and equality. Here, although the concepts of the individual and equality can be shown to be concerned with men only, they are treated as a universal truth and reality in both law and organization.

In our world, the conceptually ordered exercise of power depends upon text-based practices of communication and organization. Smith (1992) puts it this way:

Contemporary society is marked by its dependence on a certain class of communicative acts that are accorded the social capacity of standing in for, or functioning as, an actuality. They may or may not be "representational" in the sense of claiming to reproduce or picture in some way an original state of affairs. But whether they are representational or otherwise, they constitute a "virtual reality", that is a form of works, or images or numbers that can be treated as if it were the reality it stands in for – that is (a) as *independent* of the subjectivity/consciousness of any particular individual and (b) as a field or arena that is shared by members or participants *as a basis for action*, referenced by them as known in common for all practical purposes. (1; emphasis added)

Both the neutrality of the tax system and the way in which it concerts relations among people to create a social order (operates as a regime) depend upon and are constituted in practices that document a world authorized and known in common.

This world known in common is not a representation of everyday realities. It is a world constructed through and in the concepts of economics, accounting, law, and business practices. The bases for the world known in common are to be found in the technical/rational foundations of tax: the definition of tax base, the tax unit, and the rate structure. These create a domain that is objectified. The practices of administration and management that implement tax are similarly ordered to create, in text, a uniform display of what has taken place.

The text-based practices of organization and administration, known as management, are part of constituting the relations of tax, as are the professional practices of accountants, economists, and lawyers, including discussions like the one taking place in relation to fair tax in Ontario. The ubiquity of text-based practices of organization is rapidly being globalized and hence the creation of transpersonal, translocal, and transnational contexts for the exercise of power.[20]

The neutrality and uniformity of tax practices are created intertextually and aim at articulating individuals to the inherent necessities, realities, and laws of commercial relations. In tax, these relations are represented at the most general level by the conceptions of wealth, income, and consumption. These conceptions themselves have their realities and are stabilized in extended institutional text-based practices of accounting, measurement, estimation, legal definition, and professional categorization. The regime of tax, at its core, constructs a virtual reality that is not tuned to experience, but to ideological structuring that will articulate tax to the actions and consequences, at the most general level, of capital and financial markets. It is here that the power nexus is located in rational, professional, and legal terms. The work before us is to pick apart these processes to recover the way they produce the social order we live as our reality.

Equity and Fairness

In this section, I argue that equity and fairness are not the same thing. Equity is a notion that depends upon the orthodoxies of tax theory and the conceptual practices of rationality and neutrality that underpin tax administration. It does not address inequality, however much it may appear to be an improvement upon existing tax practices.

Within the discourse on tax, equity can be seen to be an attempt to address the political character of tax. The conception of equity in relation to tax formulates and attempts to implement principles of uniformity and neutrality. It seeks to ensure that similar circumstances of wealth, income, and consumption are consistently and uniformly taxed. Equity is equated with fairness.

When I was invited to prepare this paper for the Fair Tax Commission, several papers that considered equity in taxation were offered to us for consideration (Canada, Royal Commission on Taxation 1966; Meade 1978; Musgrave 1987). These reveal that two general dimensions of equity have been theorized in the public-finance literature. These dimensions are horizontal and vertical equity. The Fair Tax Commission (1992) has provided a useful summary of the positions in these papers. It formulates equity in the following manner: "Horizontal equity requires that taxpayers in similar circumstances bear the same taxes; and vertical equity requires that those taxpayers in different circumstances bear appropriately different taxes" (1).

On first consideration, these statements appear quite straightforward and commonsensical. But they are not a description that conforms or connects directly to a lived reality. Instead, they formulate two principles intended to be made into or to become a reality. Within the tax disciplines, such a formulation is a technical task. It is assumed that the task involves translating principles into categories and definitions and, finally, into forms of administration that reach into people's everyday lives so that equity is created.

There are several dimensions in the process of creating equity. First, there are theoretical assumptions about the relation between the principle, the creation of administrative forms (virtual reality), and people's lives. Second, there are the assumptions about neutrality and equality. Finally, there are the social relations among people that are organized by this process. These are the issues I want to begin to address here.

While the notions "taxpayers" and "similar circumstances" have an apparent ordinary meaning, the matter is put to the test if we go out into the world to find the lived reality that corresponds to these terms. We might expect to find that taxpayers are people and companies who pay taxes and that their similar circumstances would be self-evident. Such is not the case. These terms are, in fact, located within the technical realm of the tax disciplines. So, for example, three issues are raised in relation to creating horizontal equity: the discovery or definition of equal position, taxable units, and equal treatment (Ontario, Fair Tax Commission 1992) and one issue in relation to vertical equity, the rate structure. When we examine these issues, we find they involve making assumptions about individuals and how they behave in relation to commercial circumstances (earning/receiving and spending money) and family. The efficacy of equity in taxation is assumed to be founded on the veracity of these assumptions.

But "individuals" is a technical category. It includes those who are involved in commercial transactions – men and women who are involved in selling their labour for money, owning property, and associated activities. Moreover, individuals are not necessarily people; individuals are also business corporations in law. Tax is concerned with the commercial dimensions of individuals (how they get money and how much they get) and makes assumptions about the character of commercial relations (how they spend money). A number of behavioural assumptions from the discipline of economics underpin the creation of these categories, which are treated as a matter of fact within the theory of tax.

Feminist scholars, including Marjorie Cohen, Lousie Dullude, Martha MacDonald, and Monica Townson, have been building up a body of work that considers women in relation to and within economic analysis. With this work the examination of the conceptions of economics in relation to women is beginning to be developed. Marilyn Waring, in her book *If Women Counted: A New Feminist Economics* (1988), explores the creation of international practices of national income accounting. She notes the way in which women's work is omitted from the creation of the accounts that value the world's wealth. This brings the practices and conceptions of economics, at the most general level, into view from the perspective of women. What is evident is that the behavioural assumptions at the root of economics are not founded in the real activities of real people.

Feminist and aligned environmental critiques point to the relation to the natural world that is assumed within economic theory and business practices (Bookchin 1991; Carson 1987; Gordon 1990; Gordon and Suzuki 1990; Plant 1989). Such a relation is evident, for example, in the way the consequences of industrial activity have been and continue to be treated in business costs and in tax. More generally, environmentalists point to the exploitation, growth, efficiency, consumption, and valuation relation as central to both waste and destruction of the very world on which our physical lives depend (Hinds 1990). Both women's and environmental realities raise questions about the universe of economic relations themselves. What is treated as within and outside these relations? Why and how are relations treated in this way? How do they form everyday realities, and with what consequences? It is becoming clear that the practices of creating wealth and the definitions of wealth itself are increasingly problematic for everyday realities. They are expressed in many ways, including the tensions among state, business, and people.

We need to raise questions about the propriety of treating as fact, orthodox economic assumptions about behaviour, and about the relation of behaviour to social practices. In relation to tax, this means questioning the assumption that the definitions and categories, bear a real relation to material existence. It is my contention that, when they are based upon economic assumptions about behaviour, they are not based in everyday realities, but are concerned to make everyday realities conform to the assumptions.

Horizontal equity in tax focuses upon treating taxpayers as the same, based upon dimensions of quantity, category, and measurements of results. The practice of treating taxpayers as the same along these dimensions depends not only on definitions and assumptions discussed here, but also on administrative practices. Administrative practices begin within a virtual reality. In the context of tax, they depend upon a documentary work-up of taxpayers, and they aim at consistent and predictable treatment of the documentary work-up. In administrative terms, this is what constitutes neutrality and equal treatment. These are the aspects of the technical character of tax that create its appearance of being outside people. This "outsideness" is the product of the work activities of people.

If economics is the discipline that theorizes about and analyses economic relations, then the business/management disciplines study and contribute to the conduct of economic organization. The principles at the core of these disciplines are most generally expressed as the translocal, transpersonal character of organization (Smith 1987, 1990b; Cassin 1990, 1991). This character of organization is achieved through the creation of uniform administrative practices, which are believed to result in equitable and fair treatment/practice.[21] Feminists have been exploring the relation of organization and women's inequality. Moss Kanter (1977) displayed the location of men and women in corporations and began posing surrounding questions. Bureaucracy has been examined for how it is problematic for women. The question is being posed: Is a feminist organizational theory possible?

As women seek redress of inequality it becomes clear that practices of organization and, indeed, the apparent uniformity/neutrality of management conceptions and practices are barriers to addressing everyday realities and creating equality (Cassin 1991, 1992). Indeed the uniformity/neutrality constructed by management in organizations routinely produces (gender) inequality that is accepted as a normal dimension of our social order (Cassin 1990).

Accounting forms one of the most technical, apparently uniform, and unproblematic domains of organization. However, Elizabeth Evans (1985), in a preliminary examination of auditing, has drawn attention to the relation among auditing principles, management accounting, and the creation of women's everyday realities of inequality. Indeed, critical work in accounting is raising questions about the relation of accounting to experienced realities (Bursai 1986; Kirkham 1992; Burchell, Chubb, and Hopwood 1985; Chua 1991; Tinker, Merino, and Neimark 1982).

The routine practices of organization that treat people as the same, and are at the foundation of tax concepts of equity, have until recently been treated as both authoritative and unproblematic. Indeed, they have been seen as models for organizing equality. However, as we examine management as technologies of organization, we discover that these practices begin in men's (commercial) realities. These critiques open further the debates about the social construction of equality, how to redress inequality, and how and what constitutes gender neutrality.

We see, then, that fair or equal treatment, as formulated by equity, depends upon a work-up based on assumptions about people and their lives and administrative practices that, together, form a virtual reality. This is treated as equivalent to fairness in everyday life. For this sort of practice to work in relation to the lives of people, the assumptions must be embedded in everyday realities, and the administrative practice needs to be designed to attend to those realities. A simple examination of notions about the tax base offers further illustration.

In the case of individual persons, salary income as a basis for tax is quite straightforward and easily accessible by government. Tax is deducted at source by employers. People in this situation have no need of tax specialists or accountants, since they are not in a position to negotiate matters of tax.

The income of business is not similarly direct. Determining corporate tax is the product of an elaborate organizational process that includes accounting; auditing; and conceptions and definitions of costs, revenue, profits, tax law, and accounting theory. Business income is generally less accessible to tax than salary income, as is apparent in the different contributions to government income – individuals pay a larger share than do businesses.

Corporate tax practices and tax accounting can be usefully examined using methods of inquiry from feminism and, in particular, new materialism. The presentation of the affairs of a corporation for the purpose of tax is a different matter from the presentation of salary income. The resources and efforts expended to place an organization in the most advantageous tax positions are considerable. Similarly, individuals with substantial resources arrange their affairs to gain tax advantage. Indeed, this goal and activity provide work for the accounting divisions of accounting and management consulting firms.

Tax specialists have long recognized that taxes have effects upon people and businesses. Taxes are based upon assumptions about people and businesses. They organize our relations with one another. Tax is a social relation; that is, our relations with one another are not organized directly, but through the extended practice of determining, organizing, and collecting tax. Although tax is seen to provide for common needs, being taxpayers seems to organize a common antagonism to state and politics. Moreover, as taxpayers, it seems we have interests in common. But when we look more closely, all taxpayers do not share a common interest.

Feminist critique shows us that conceptions of the individual and equality are matters of social organization theorized in knowledge and practised in definite ways in the institutional organization of our society. In general, these concepts and practices rule women and set the conditions of our lives, but do not include us in their making. The feminine is characterized as different and apart from, and in opposition to rationality.

There are problems with treating people the same when that "sameness" is created by virtual realities (bureaucratic administration, professional categorization, managerial technology, and so on). There are also problems with equating this "same" treatment with fairness and equality. Although the view of the Canadian courts is not yet clear, the exploration of equality and inequality in relation to women has brought into view the restrictive character of conventional conceptions of equality. The practices of treating people the same when their circumstances are different has come to be recognized in scholarship as a contribution to the organization of inequality.

I take a similar view of equity. In relation to women's pay, equity is seen by management to be achieved by treating jobs as the same through job evaluation. In this context, equity is a management-based concept. However, job evaluation is based upon sex-based categorizations of occupations, gendered practices of creating job documentation, an ideological creation of "measurement," and a spurious minimizing objectification of women's work (Armstrong 1984; Cassin 1988, 1990, 1991). Feminists are currently at work picking job evaluation apart to find a way in which to reorder the basis of pay and the relations of men's and women's work. An equally rigorous examination of the economics- and accounting-based concept and practice of equity in tax must be undertaken. Tax practices are not currently rooted in a science connected to everyday life. Instead, they are embedded in a virtual reality that seeks to rule everyday life. Fairness cannot be gained through such practices.

Widening the Circle

So what of fairness in relation to tax? In the first place, equity, as it is currently thought of and defined, does not constitute fairness from the location of everyday social realities. We need to pursue the development of a conception of fairness and associated practice by opening tax and equity to an interrogation from everyday social realities. We need to widen the scope of what it might mean to have fairness in tax.

This process involves the ongoing investigation, debate, and design of tax measures and tax monitoring. We need to take seriously the requirement for empirical interrogation of the conceptions of the categories of tax in relation to the categories and operation of business/commercial practices and the everyday realities of men and women, including matters of race, sexual preference, conscience, disability, and environment. We need to use the innovative methods of investigation being developed in the social and managerial sciences and in feminism. In particular, the advent of critical work in accounting that examines the social organization of accounting, which I have already mentioned, has much to teach us about business and tax from the location of lived realities. Persons other than economists and accountants need to study these matters to broaden the scope of the discussion beyond business/commerce.

These are ways of learning about and coming to address the relations of power inherent in and organized by tax. We need to make tax open to public debate. This work gives us the ground to articulate the social values and principles and practices that need to be at the foundation of our tax, as they need to be at the foundation of our social order.

Notes

The first draft of this study was prepared for the Ontario Fair Tax Commission and completed in February 1992.

1 This notion is borrowed from feminist lawyers who work in the Women's Legal Education and Action Fund (LEAF). In that context, it formulates the need to broaden the scope of existing institutional knowledge to include the realities of women's lives as a basis for institutional action and decision making.

2 Dobbin bases his work on research published by Canadian academics (including economists, political scientists, accountants, and lawyers), and interviews with journalists, politicians, businessmen, academics, and tax specialists. The reading lists and transcript are available through CBC "Ideas," Box 500, Station "A," Toronto, Ontario, M5W 1E6.

3 Dobbin points out that even when there has been broad-based popular opposition, as in the case of the introduction of the GST in Canada, this opposition has been ignored in favour of the interests represented by the tax community.

4 This approach and argument in this section is informed by the work of Dorothy E. Smith, in particular, her work in developing a sociology for women entitled *The Everyday World as Problematic: A Feminist Sociology*. The title of the section is taken from the title of her book.

5 It is expected that the recent changes to the tax system organized by the current government will intensify this distribution of the tax burden so that women will bear increasingly more tax. This is ironic in view of the interest in poverty, particularly child poverty. It needs to

be noted that child poverty is, of course, a direct expression of the economic circumstances (including tax burden) of women.

6 By the facts, I mean the institutional data about women and tax.

7 The following exposition of the critical and epistemological developments in feminist scholarship are drawn from the work of Simone de Beauvoir.

8 The reference is to Dorothy Smith (1987) who uses the term to focus upon the way in which women disappear from both science and places of authority in the social order.

9 Objectivity has become a subject of investigation in more than feminism. Indeed, in feminist sociology, we are deeply indebted to ethnomethodology (in particular, the work of Garfinkel [1967]), a field in sociology that makes problematic everyday, professional, and scientific practices of organization, reasoning, and knowledge.

10 During the seminar (Fair Tax Commission, 26 February, 1992) that was held to discuss these papers, Margrit Eichler and a number of tax specialists had a fascinating exchange. These exchanges are essential (in both face-to-face and textual forms) to begin to inform tax specialists of social realities and explore tax changes.

11 The term comes from Lahey's work and will be discussed further in this section.

12 The Supreme Court of Canada has recently granted leave to appeal the decision of the Federal Court of Appeal (A-290-89). The Respondent's Memorandum of Fact and Law prepared for the Federal Court of Appeal and the Applicant's Memorandum of Argument for the Supreme Court of Canada provide important insights into both corporations and tax, and the situation of women in business. I am indebted to Mary Eberts, counsel for Ms Symes, for providing me with the documents and for her discussions with me of her views on the issues surrounding women and corporate tax.

13 Stevenson 1986.

14 This case has given rise to a debate about gender and class among feminist legal scholars. Some feminist legal scholars have raised questions about the propriety of allowing business expenses of any kind as a deduction.

15 This has been accompanied by initiatives both to offer education for judges and to encourage the appointment of women to the bench. It is generally felt that the decisions and legal reflections of Madam Justice Bertha Wilson are exemplary in relation to bringing women's perspective to bear in a broad range of legal thinking (1991 Symposium, Dalhousie University Law School).

16 It should be noted that there is, of course, a debate about whether or not this is a workable strategy, which is discussed admirably by Sherene Razack (1990) in her book.

17 A similar process, although not as well theorized, can be seen to be at work in the consideration of equity and gender neutrality in relation to pay currently being adjudicated through administrative tribunal and negotiated in labour relations.

18 This section draws upon Smith's work in specifying the practice of institutional organizations in our society and, in particular, on her work on textual analysis (1990a, 1990b). The title of the section is taken from the title of her book, *The Conceptual Practices of Power: A Feminist Sociology of Knowledge* (1990a).

19 I use the term "technology" in the way formulated by Ursula Franklin in her book *The Real World of Technology* (1990). She formulates technology as more than technical capacities. She sees technology as ways of doing things that order and organize the relations of people with one another.

20 This poses the practical problems of trying to implement new ideas and practices in single jurisdictions.

21 The study of organizations is now spread through a number of disciplines, including sociology and management, but the practitioner relation is organized through the management disciplines.

Bibliography

Armstrong, P. 1974. *The Double Ghetto: Canadian Women and Their Segregated Work.* Toronto: McClelland and Stewart
– 1984. *Labour Pains: Women's Work in Crisis.* Toronto: Women's Press
Armstrong, P., and H. Armstrong. 1984. *The Double Ghetto: Canadian Women and Their Segregated Work,* rev. ed. Toronto: McClelland and Stewart
Axworthy, Thomas S. 1987. "Liberalism and Equality." In *Equality and Judicial Neutrality,* ed. Sheilah L. Martin and Kathleen Mahoney, 43–9. Toronto: Carswell
Baxter, W.T. 1989. "Early Accounting: The Tally and the Checkerboard." *Accounting Historians Journal,* 16 (2): 43–86
Bayevsky, Anne. 1985. "Defining Equality Rights." In *Equality Rights and the Canadian Charter of Rights and Freedoms,* ed. Anne Bayevsky and Mary Eberts, 1–79. Toronto: Carswell

Beauchesne, Eric. 1989. "Family Tax Bite Getting Bigger." *Chronicle Herald,* 11 April 1989

Benston, Margret. 1974. "The Double Day of Labour." *Catalyst,* 6 (2): 164–71

Berger, Margret. 1980. "Litigation on Behalf of Women." Review for the Ford Foundation. May

Bookchin, Murray. 1991. *The Ecology of Freedom,* rev. ed. Montreal: Black Rose

Boyle, Christine. 1985a. "Sexual Assault and the Feminist Judge." *Canadian Journal of Women and the Law,* 1: 93–107

– 1985b. *Sexual Assault.* Toronto: Carswell

– 1989. "A Feminist Approach to Criminal Defences." Typescript

Boyle, Christine, and Sheila Noonan. 1986 "Prostitution and Pornography: Beyond Formal Equality." In *Charterwatch: Refelections on Equality,* ed. Christine Boyle, A. Wayne MacKay, Edward J. McBride, and John A. Yogis, 225–65. Toronto: Carswell

Burchell, S., C. Chubb, and A.G. Hopwood. 1985. "Accounting in Its Social Context: Toward a History of Value Added in the United Kingdom." In *Accounting, Organizations and Society,* 6 (2): 381–414

Bursai, Nasuhi. 1986. "The Use of Interest as an Element of Cost in Germany in the 16th and 17th Centuries." *Accounting Historians Journal,* 13 (1): 63–86

Burstyn, Varda, and Dorothy E. Smith. 1985. *Women, Class, Family and State.* Toronto: Garamond Press

Canada. Royal Commission on Taxation. 1966. *Report,* Vols. 1 and 2. Ottawa: Queen's Printer

– Royal Commission on the Status of Women in Canada. 1970. *Report.* Ottawa: Information Canada

Carson, Rachel. 1987. *Silent Spring.* Boston: Houghton Mifflin

Cassin, A. Marguerite. 1987. "Women and Education." Affidavit Testimony, 29 January (Supreme Court of Ontario), *FWTAO v. Tomen*

– 1988. "Affirmative Action: Implications for Women and Equality." Typescript

– 1990. "The Routine Production of Inequality: A Study in the Social Organization of Knowledge." PhD dissertation, University of Toronto, Ontario Institute for Studies in Education

– 1991. *Women, Work, Jobs and Value: The Routine Production of Inequality.* A Report with special reference to Consumers" Gas Expert testimony before the Ontario Pay Equity Tribunal

– 1992. Expert testimony before the Ontario Pay Equity Tribunal. April

Christophersen, Dale. 1977. "The Concept of Equality: An Analysis and Justification." PhD dissertation, University of Missouri, Columbia

Chua, Wai Fong. 1991. "The Social Manufacture of Hospital Costs." Paper presented at the Third International Perspectives on Accounting Conference, University of Manchester, July

Cooper, R., and R.S. Kaplan. 1987. "How Cost Accounting Systematically Distorts Production Costs." In *Accounting and Management: Field Study Perspectives*, ed. W.J. Bruns and R.S. Caplain, 204–28. Cambridge, MA: Harvard Business School Press

Eberts, Mary. 1985a. "Making Use of the Charter of Rights." In *Women, the Law and the Economy*, ed. Diane E. Pask, Kathleen E. Mahoney, and Catherine A. Brown, 327–48. Toronto: Butterworths

– 1985b. "The Use of Litigation under the Canadian Charter of Rights and Freedoms." In *Minorities and the Canadian State*, ed. Neil Nevitte and Allan Kornberg, 53–69. Oakville, ON: Mosaic Press

– 1986. "A Strategy for Equality Litigation under the Canadian Charter of Rights and Freedoms." In *Litigating the Values of a Nation: The Canadian Charter of Rights and Freedoms*, ed. Joseph M. Weiler and Robin M. Elliot, 411–26. Toronto: Carswell

– 1987. "Risks of Equality Litigation." In *Equality and Judicial Neutrality*, ed. Sheilah L. Martin and Kathleen Mahoney, 89–105. Toronto: Carswell

– 1991. "New Facts for Old: Observations on the Judicial Process." In *Canadian Perspectives on Legal Theory*, ed. Richard F. Devlin, 467–502. Toronto: E. Montgomery Publications

Eichler, Margrit. 1988. *Families in Canada Today: Recent Changes and Their Political Consequences*, 2d ed. Toronto: Gage

Evans, Elizabeth. 1985. "Accounting for Stichco." Graduate paper, University of Toronto, Ontario Institute for Studies in Education

Franklin, Ursula. 1990. *The Real World of Technology*. Toronto: CBC Enterprises

Gallighar, Janet. 1987. "Prenatal Invasions & Interventions: What's Wrong with Fetal Rights." *Harvard Women's Law Journal*, 10: 9–58

Garfinkel, Harold. 1967. "'Good' Organizational Reasons for 'Bad' Clinical Records." In *Ethnomethodology*, ed. Roy Turner, 109–27. Harmondsworth: Penguin Education

Gavigan, Shelley A.M. 1986. "Women, Law and Patriarchal Relations: Perspectives within the Sociology of Law." In *The Social Dimensions of Law*, ed. Neil Boyd, 101–24. Scarborough: Prentice-Hall Canada

Goode, E.L. 1982. "Conceptions of Economy." Typescript

Gordon, Anita, and David Suzuki. 1990. *It's a Matter of Survival*. Toronto: Stoddart

Gordon, David, ed. 1990. *Green Cities: Ecologically Sound Approaches to Urban Space*. Montreal: Black Rose Books

Griffith, Alison I. 1984. "Ideology, Education and Single Parent Families:

The Normative Ordering of Families through Schooling." PhD dissertation, University of Toronto

– 1986. "Constructing Cultural Knowledge: Mothering as Discourse." Paper presented at the Mothering and Education Conference, University of British Columbia

Griffith, Alison I., and Dorothy E. Smith. 1985. "Coordinating the Uncoordinated: How Mothers Manage the School Day." Paper presented at the American Sociological Association, Washington, DC, August

Hacker, Sally L. 1990. *Doing It the Hard Way: Investigations of Gender and Technology.* Boston: Unwin Hyman

Hale, Sylvia M. 1990. *Controversies in Sociology: A Canadian Introduction.* Toronto: Copp Clark Pitman

Harding, Sandra. 1986. *The Science Question in Feminism.* Ithaca, NY: Cornell University Press

Hinds, Ruth D. 1992. "Accounting: Filling the Negative Space." *Accounting, Organizations and Society,* 17 (3–4): 1313–41

Institute for Fiscal Studies. 1978. *The Structure and Reform of Direct Taxation. Report of a Committee chaired by Prof. J.E. Meade* (Meade Report). London: Allen and Unwin

Kanter, Rosabeth Moss. 1977. *Men and Women and the Corporation.* New York: Basic Books

Keller, Evelyn Fox. 1985. *Reflections on Gender and Science.* New Haven, CT: Yale University Press

Kirkham, Linda M. 1992. "Integrating Herstory and History in Accounting." *Accounting, Organization and Society,* 17 (3–4): 287–97

Lahey, Kathleen A. 1987. "Feminist Theories of (In)Equality." In *Equality and Judicial Neutrality,* ed. Sheilah L. Martin and Kathleen Mahoney, 71–85. Toronto: Carswell

– 1988a. "Civil Remedies for Women: Catching the Critical Edge." *Resources for Feminist Research/Documentation sur la recherche feministe,* 17 (3): 92–5

– 1988b. "The Taxation of Women in Canada: A Research Report." Unpublished manuscript

Luxton, Meg. 1980. *More Than a Labour of Love: Three Generations of Women's Work in the Home.* Toronto: Womens Press

MacKinnon, Catharine A. 1987. *Feminism Unmodified: Discourses on Life and Law.* Cambridge, MA: Harvard University Press

Manicom, Ann. 1988. "The Reproduction of Class: The Relation between Two Work Processes." PhD dissertation, University of Toronto

Meade Report. *See* Institute for Fiscal Studies

Mills, Patti, A. 1987. "The Probative Capacity of Accounts in Early-Modern Spain." *Accounting Historians Journal,* 14 (1): 95–108

Mossman, Mary Jane. 1986. "Feminism and Legal Method: The Difference It Makes." *Australian Journal of Law and Society*, 3: 30–52

Murphy, George J. 1986. "A Chronology of the Development of Corporate Financial Reporting in Canada: 1850–1983." *Accounting Historians Journal*, 13 (1): 31–61

– 1988. *The Evolution of Selected Annual Corporate Financial Reporting Practices in Canada 1900–1970.* New York: Garland

Musgrave, Richard A. 1983. "The Nature of Horizontal Equity and the Principle of Broad-Based Taxation: A Friendly Critique." In *Taxations Issues of the 1980s*, ed. John G. Head, 21–23. Sydney: Australian Tax Research Foundation

– 1987. "Equity Principles in Public Finance." In *The Relevance of Public Finance for Policy-Making*, ed. Hans M. van de Kar and B.L. Wolfe, 113–23. Detroit: Wayne State University Press

New Brunswick. 1990. *"What Comes First?" A Report on the Payment of Support Orders in New Brunswick.* Moncton: Advisory Council on the Status of Women

Nova Scotia. 1989. *"Where Is Inequity?" A comparison of tax paid by two-earner families that use child care and one-earner families with pre-school children at home.* Halifax: Advisory Council on the Status of Women

Oakley, Ann. 1974. *The Sociology of Housework.* London: Martin Robertson

O'Brien, Mary, and Sheila McIntyre. 1986. "Patriarchal Hegemony and Legal Education." *Canadian Journal of Women and the Law*, 2 (1): 69–95

Ontario. Fair Tax Commission. 1992. "Equity Principles in Taxation." Unpublished discussion paper

Pietilä, Hilkka. 1985. "Tomorrow Begins Today." ICDA/ISIS Workshop in Forum, Nairobi

Plant, Judith, ed. 1989. *Healing the Wounds.* Toronto: Between the Lines

Razack, Sherene. 1990. *Canadian Feminism and the Law.* Toronto: Second Story Press

Sheehy, Elizabeth. 1987. *Personal Autonomy and the Criminal Law: Emerging Issues for Women.* Ottawa: Canadian Advisory Council on the Status of Women

Smith, Dorothy E. 1987. *The Everyday World as Problematic: A Feminist Sociology.* Toronto: University of Toronto Press

– 1990a. The *Conceptual Practices of Power: A Feminist Sociology of Knowledge.* Toronto: University of Toronto Press

– 1990b. *Texts, Facts and Femininity: Exploring the Relations of Ruling.* London; New York: Routledge

– 1992. "Whistling Women." In *Fragile Truths: Twenty-five Years of Sociology and Anthropology in Canada*, ed. William K. Carroll, 208–26. Ottawa: Carleton University Press

Stevenson, Lois. 1986. "Women Business Owners: Common Myths." *Proceedings*, Atlantic Schools of Business Conference

Symes, Beth. 1987. "Equality Theories and Maternity Benefits." In *Equality and Judicial Neutrality*, ed. Sheilah L. Martin and Kathleen Mahoney, 207–17. Toronto: Carswell

Tinker, A.M., B.D. Merino, and M. Neimark. 1982. "The Normative Origins of Positive Accounting: Ideology and Accounting Thought." *Accounting Organizations and Society*, 3(1): 167–200

Van Dyke, Vernon. 1990. *Equality and Public Policy*. Chicago: Nelson-Hall

Walsh, Larry. 1989. "GST Will Cost 180,000 Jobs, Woman's Group Tells Hearing," *Chronicle Herald*, 3 October 1989

Waring, Marilyn. 1988. *If Women Counted: A New Feminist Economics*. New York: HarperCollins

5 Beyond the Crisis of the Tax State?

From Fair Taxation to Structural Reform

LEO PANITCH

> Taxes not only helped to create the state. They helped to form it ... The kind and level of taxes are determined by the social structure, but once taxes exist they become a handle, as it were, which social powers can grip in order to change this structure. (Schumpeter 1991, 108).

Introduction: States and Taxes

Historically speaking, death and taxes really do go together, at least in the form of the couplet of war and income tax. The first introduction of income tax under Pitt in England at the very end of the 18th century was occasioned by the Napoleonic Wars. (Notably, Pitt tried to justify this tax in terms that tax experts today would call "horizontal equity" – a shilling is a shilling? – by arguing that it was in order "to prevent all evasion and fraud" that "a general tax shall be imposed on the leading branches of income.")[1] The modern system of income tax traces its roots in Britain, Canada, and the United States to the First World War, and its contemporary structure emerges in the Second World War, during which time it moved from being a tax mainly on the upper classes and became a graduated tax on the mass of incomes. The relationship is by no means circumstantial: it evolves in a dialectic between the massive expansion of state expenditure during war, on the one hand, and the plausibility of an appeal to the value of social commitment rather than mere egoism at a time of national mobilization for war, on the other.

But there is a third element at play at each of these historical moments: democracy. This took the form of the radical ideas of the

French Revolution in Pitt's time, the emergence of mass working parties and unions, and the accelerating demands for extension of the suffrage around the start of the First World War, and the struggle for mass unionization and collective bargaining around that of the Second World War. In each case, the class compromises struck through the state, in the context of dominant class fear of these challeges from below and a strategy to contain them, together with the need for mobilization of mass support at moments of national crisis, provided the political conditions for extensive reforms in state finance. The lesson this teaches is this: "Taxation, while intrinsically a matter of social and economic policy, is best understood politically, as something that is first and foremost a matter of setting agendas and building coalitions and only secondarily a matter of finding the best way to finance expenditure ... Understanding the shifting politics of taxation, then, is essential to understanding the social character of the state and the possibilities for social and economic policy in the polity."[2]

The Crisis of Progressive Taxation

An unmistakable general trend in the structure of public finance emerged right across the advanced capitalist countries during the 1980s. In the words of a leading Organization for Economic Cooperation and Development (OECD) public-finance expert: "vertical equity has been thrown out of the tax policy door."[3] If not exactly thrown out the door, then at least made to feel distinctly unwelcome has been the advocate of "progressive" taxation who argues that taxes should rest on a graduated ability-to-pay basis; and, relatedly, that this tax regime should contribute to promoting a significant measure of income and/or wealth redistribution. As for the traditional tax policy trade-off between the promotion of social goals and the promotion of the idea of tax neutrality vis-à-vis the economy, the same observer has noted that tax neutrality is "now predominating except in certain sensitive areas." In this context, even horizontal equity is no longer defined in tax policy discourse as it once was (most famously in Canada by the Carter Report, 1966) as a means of fashioning a comprehensive income concept that would justify bringing capital gains and wealth transfers within the purview of progressive taxation. Rather, it is now defined more as a means of guaranteeing minimum public interference: both with the investment and distributional outcomes of uncontrolled markets, and with the decisional prerogatives of the hierarchically structured private corporations that are the main actors in them. An old historic truth has once again become clear: bound up with the issue of equity in taxation is the broader issue of the proper relationship between capitalism and democracy.

The recent changes in the structure of tax regimes is commonly seen as part and parcel of a coherent neoliberal strategy of disengaging markets from state intervention. This was epitomized by the tax reforms of the Thatcher and Reagan administrations – into which ideological mould may also be fitted the Mulroney government's major tax reforms along the lines outlined by Allan Maslove (1989, esp. 24–5) in his account of tax reform and the Tory agenda. Of course, one must not overemphasize the actual degree of change such governments have wrought. They took hold in tax regimes that, once all forms of taxation were aggregated, were never very progressive or much more than proportional in their effects, in any case; and which, not least through a pot-pourri of special allowances for investors over the previous decade, already had become (depending on your favoured definition of tax incidence) either less progressive or more regressive.[4] Although the main thrust of the 1980s reforms was to simplify and broaden the tax base by trading off some specific tax incentives for lower marginal rates of income tax and a further accelerated shift to consumption taxes, many tax allowances were still permitted to continue. To some extent, the revolution wrought by neoconservatism was primarily ideological: throwing vertical equity out the door was a gesture that entailed making a virtue of what previous regimes had hidden away or had treated as a regretted necessity. And to the extent that we may properly say that neoconservatism had actual material as well as ideological effects, explanations in terms of a coherent philosophy of government on the political right should not blind us to the importance of the cruder concerns that always motivate parties of business, whose "historical role has been not simply to revitalize ... capitalism, but to tilt power, wealth and income towards the richest portions of the population."[5]

Yet it would be a serious misunderstanding to see recent changes in tax regimes only in terms of the politics of the right. What is particularly striking and important about the trend towards throwing vertical equity out the tax-policy window is its generality, the very fact that it is not confined to governments of neoconservative ideological persuasion based on parties organically rooted in the world of business. Even in countries where parties of the labourist and social-democratic left have occupied or shared office in the 1980s,

including Australia, New Zealand, France, Germany, the Nether-
lands, Denmark, and, most notably, Sweden, governments have introduced tax changes that reflected the same trend. What this suggests
is that something more structural, more profoundly historical, has
been happening.

If the recognition of this more fundamental problem makes the task
set before the Ontario Fair Tax Commission – to determine how to
design and implement a more equitable tax system – seem all the
more enormous, it also suggests at the same time that the commission's findings and effects, if they are positive, may well have exemplary significance not only beyond the province and Canada but
also beyond the era of neoconservatism. In May 1989, when Floyd
Laughren, at the time the opposition Treasury and Finance critic,
issued his *Made in Ontario: A Fairer Tax System*, a document that called
for a separate personal income tax system in Ontario along the lines
of that in Quebec, a wealth tax, and a minimum corporate tax, his
prime motivation was, to borrow a phrase from the accompanying
press release, "a much more progressive tax structure."[6] Although he
invited the government of Ontario to get on the "bandwagon" of the
22 of 24 OECD countries that administered an annual net-wealth tax
or estate tax at death, it was in fact the New Democratic Party (NDP)
that was then, consciously or not, getting off the bandwagon of most
OECD countries, including those governed at the time by its sister
social-democratic parties, who were showing vertical-tax-equity advocacy the door at this very time.

The issue of taxation as cast by the NDP, alongside a broad popular
demand for a more honest, open, and democratic form of government
(the two issues may indeed be closely related), figured prominently
in the campaign that brought the NDP to office in the first major
electoral victory by a party of the left in an advanced capitalist country
in almost a decade. Most notable of all, perhaps, was the fact that
the first major public speech of the new Treasurer of Ontario involved
his going into the den of the Canadian Tax Foundation's annual conference and avowing that he had always been "impressed with the
clarity" of the Carter Report's view on tax fairness (Laughren 1991).
Whatever one may think of the actual clarity of the Carter Report in
this respect, its courageous ranking of equity over all other competing
tax goals, and its substantive reach towards greater taxation of the
most wealthy and powerful, could not stand in more explicit contrast
with the international trend of the 1980s in tax policy.

If the Fair Tax Comission is to fulfil its mandate, it will need to go beyond the Carter Report by devising a viable new strategy for actually achieving a substantive measure of vertical equity. Doing so will entail establishing the case for values alternative to neoconservative and neoliberal ones. This need not prove too difficult to do. As the OECD's Kenneth Messere (1988, 281) put it: "Though by definition equity issues involve value judgements, they seem to me more clearly defined than issues relating to economic efficiency and simplicity, which are systematically ambiguous and change over time." But it will not be enough to reassert traditional egalitarian values of distributive justice in an era when social-democratic governments have recently retreated from them. It will be necessary to investigate and arrive at an understanding of the structural factors that underlay the generality of the trend away from vertical equity. This understanding will have to be a historical one, one that reveals the way changes in capitalism itself – above all, the re-emergence of tendencies to crisis over the past quarter-century – have forced this emphasis on efficiency to the detriment of equity. Although this still allowed for some real scope for manoeuvre, depending on the ideological colouration and social base of the parties in governmental office, there may have been little alternative to the general trend within the limits of the traditional relationship between the liberal democratic state and the private market economy. In other words, to achieve an equitable structural reform in a tax regime today is very likely going to mean structural reforms in the state as well as in the economy, and in the relationship between them.

It is important to begin by trying to arrive at an understanding of what meaning might be attributed to the rather ambiguous notion of fair taxation. It is to help the commission clarify this notion that this paper has been commissioned, and it shall accordingly concern itself mainly with that question. But this paper is written with the understanding that values are only a guide to the action that makes them effective. The next step should be to turn to history as seen through the eyes of political economy and political sociology to appreciate why the scope for implementing such values was opened up in an earlier era and then contracted again so considerably in our time. Only then can we begin to see the outlines of what is needed today by way of a viable political strategy for democratic-egalitarian structural reform. We will briefly address these historical and strategic issues in the concluding section of this paper.

"Fair Taxation": Getting beyond Appearances

Marx (1959, III: 797–8) once referred to certain concepts as being "just as irrational as a yellow logarithm." He had in mind concepts (such as the "price of labour") that might be commonly used in everyday life, but that reflected only life's outward appearances while actually concealing the social, economic, and political relations that structure our lives. Since "all science would be superfluous if the outward appearance and the essence of things directly coincided," those economists who did no more than "interpret, systematize and defend in doctrinaire fashion" the conceptions conventionally employed in the economy were engaged in a vulgarization of social-scientific practice.

There is a certain sense in which "fair taxation" may qualify conceptually as a "yellow logarithm." Although the notion might be thought to have various rather problematic aspects,[6] the main one is that the concept of "fair taxes" may obscure the essential point that the standard of what is fair inheres not in the system of taxation itself, but only in that system's relation to the system of distribution of income and wealth in the society. Musgrave appropriately quotes Wicksell in this respect: "It is clear that justice in taxation presupposes justice in the existing distribution of property and income."[7] But it is precisely the latter that we may not "presuppose" to be just – so we must address this issue before the concept of fair taxes can make sense. Moroever, it will not be possible to assess fair-taxes proposals and strategies themselves and what they might actually accomplish so long as we avoid the question of the nature and significance of the power relations which lie behind the existing distribution of income and wealth. It is only to the extent that a conception of fair taxes can be outfitted with a theory of justice and a theory of power that we can be confident that it may be made serviceable for analytic and strategic purposes rather than mystifying ones.

Since the relevant referent must be the existing distribution of property and income, let us start there. We are invited by various statistical techniques to apprehend this distribution in linear and graduated terms, whether expressed in quintile distributions, Gini coefficients, or Lorenz curves. These means of representation are not the stuff of pot-boilers, but they can be quite arresting as regards the degree of inequality in our society. (Such as those that reveal that, in 1989, before transfers and taxes, the lowest quintile of families and unattached individuals received only 1.2 per cent of total income, the second quintile only 8.7 per cent, and the third only 16.9 per cent;

in contrast with the share of just under 27 per cent thereby accounted for by the bottom 60 per cent, the top quintile alone were the recipients of no less than 47.2 per cent of total income.)[8]

A most revealing mode of representation of income inequality is the Dutch economist Jan Pen's brilliantly conceived "Parade of Dwarfs (and a few Giants)." Pen organized for the readers of his book, *Income Distribution* (1971, 48–53), a parade of all individual income recipients in Britain. He produced a spectacular effect by imitating the Greek god Procrustes, who was capable of stretching or contracting his house guests to fit the size of his bed. For his own purposes, Pen adjusted the height of the marchers to match their respective incomes (relative to the average income recipient who is given the average height). The parade moves at a uniform speed so that it passes in one hour. I have described this parade in my introductory lectures for 20 years to excite students' interest in the subject of inequality; it may be worth while to offer a glimpse of it here for the reader's edification.

The parade begins tragi-comically with people of negative height. ("On closer inspection they prove to be businessmen who have suffered losses and whose capital is reduced. They are not necessarily short people. In fact right in front we spot a few very tall men, with their feet on the ground and their heads deep in the earth. The first one may be as tall as ten yards – he must be rich to indulge in that kind of thing. It's an unhealthy thing and most of them don't keep it up for long.") It quickly moves on to people the size of matchsticks (boys with paper rounds, housewives who have worked a short time for some money). After five minutes, it suddenly jumps to those who look more like real people, a heterogenous group of dwarfs about three feet high: some young women who work in factories, but mostly people not in paid work, like pensioners, divorced women without alimony, people with a physical handicap, shopkeepers doing a poor trade, artists whose genius has not yet been recognized by the gallery owners. Only after ten minutes do we see mainly full-time workers, but all of them are still very short since they are in low-paid occupations defined as unskilled; a great many of these people are women ("precisely among these lower-paid categories each group applies the principle of ladies first"). Even after fifteen minutes, "we keep on seeing dwarfs. Of course they gradually become a little taller, but it is a slow process. They include masses of workers, just ordinary people with not inconsiderable technical knowledge, but shorties."

If we were expecting to see people of average height after half an hour, we were mistaken: they do not appear before us until only 12 minutes are left. In the six minutes it takes for people of average height to pass, we see teachers, executive-class civil servants, insurance agents, foremen, superintendents, and technicians. Only after this, with six minutes left in the parade, come the top 10 per cent, wherein we see passing before us people who start at six feet six inches high, but many have quite modest jobs: headmasters; small contractors; seamen; some farmers – people who never really thought of themselves in the top 10 per cent. I will let Pen (1971, 48–53) take it from here:

> In the last few minutes, giants suddenly loom up. A lawyer, not particularly successful: eighteen feet tall. A colonel, also of much the same height. Engineers who work for nationalized industries. The first doctors come into sight, seven to eight yards, the first accountants. There is still one minute to go, and we now see towering fellows. University professors, nine yards, senior officers of large concerns, ten yards, a Permanent Secretary thirteen yards tall, and an even taller High Court judge; a few accountants ... and surgeons of twenty yards or more. This category also includes managers of nationalized concerns: the Chairman of the National Coal Board is likewise a good twenty yards. During the last few seconds the scene is dominated by colossal figures: people like tower flats. Most of them prove to be businessmen, managers of large firms and holders of many directorships, and also film stars and a few members of the Royal Family ... But the rear of the parade is brought up by a few participants who are measured in miles ... Most of them are men of venerable age, but they also include women; these are as a rule younger and we even think that we can see a few babies and adolescents. These super-rich people are almost all heirs, and the tallest of them have managed to multiply their inheritance. The last man, whose back we can still see long after the parade had passed by, is John Paul Getty ... His height is inconceivable: at least ten miles, and perhaps twice as much.

If we tried to replicate the parade for Canada today, it would certainly look different, but how different? Perhaps the commission will try it for Ontario: it would serve to present the income distibution to which fair taxes are supposed to address themselves in a manner that really says something. Of course, no matter how impressive the means of representation, what would still be required is an explanation of the pattern of the distribution. Pen presents his parade at the start of a chapter entitled "Some Facts to Be Explained."

Such an explanation would have to be complex and nuanced. At its core would have to be access to management and ultimately ownership of capital, although it is apparent that there must be much else going on (including age and gender) that distinguishes the order in which below-average incomes appear in the parade. Access to capital may be broadly enough understood so that it encompasses those who get the opportunity to work as distinguished from those marginalized in the labour market. But certainly as regards the "shattering impression" made by the inequalities represented at the end of the parade, those whose incomes are so great as to shift most other people into dwarf-like income status, we are dealing primarily with the fruits of accumulation: "the source is always profits" avers Pen (who is little given to exaggerating the significance of capital for the general picture of inequality). Although those with some capital and income from profits can be found anywhere along the parade, there can be no understanding of the distribution at the top that does not dwell on how capital comes to be managed and owned by some people, and what it entails in terms of power over others.

What all linear representations of income inequality obscure, even Pen's wonderful parade, is that real people are not arranged in society on a ladder or marching on a linear path: there is a set of determining relationships among the income recipients; their incomes are not earned in isolation from one another. We do not see our marchers in exchange with one another, nor do we see them at work, taking or giving orders. Yet those at the top tend to be the ones with the decisional prerogative to determine who works on what, where, and how. Most important, the wealth of those with these prerogatives is augmented not only by buying cheap and selling dear, and not only by the temporary monopoly of entrepreneurial innovation, but also by what C.B. Macpherson (1973) properly called "a net transfer of powers" from those who work with nature and technology to produce goods and services but who can lay no claim, by virtue of property rights and the conditions of the labour contract, to the capital values they thereby augment through their creative powers.

What Is Fair in Public Finance?

Discussions of equity in traditional public-finance literature unfortunately bother themselves little with either explanations of or justifications for "the existing distribution of property and income." That is not to say they are unaware of the power that inheres in capital.

Both the Meade Report (1981) and Musgrave (1981 and 1987) offer clear insights into this power in their discussion of how tax inequities are capitalized. Both are perhaps a bit too ready to identify the efficiency constraint on tax policy with a broad incentive that capitalists must have to risk investment. At the very least it may be said that they fail to recognize what such a constraint really tells us about undemocratic economic and political power in so far as the state, communities, workers, and citizens depend so abjectly on what capitalists do with their ownership or control of most of the society's productive capacity. Their concentration on horizontal equity, while opening the door to a broad-based tax system that includes taxes on capital, really rests on one of the oldest of capitalists" requirements of the state: that it treat all capitals equally so as to maintain the conditions of competition. It is unfortunate that their discussions of efficiency ignore that well-documented tendency for overinvestment, which tax incentives (except those which are explicitly counter-cyclical) presumably encourage: can a theory, which cannot account for the causes of economic crises, provide a sound account of the proper role of public finance?

The horizontal- and vertical-equity yardsticks employed by the Carter Report, much influenced by Musgrave's writings on public finance,[9] remain admirable in their insistence that people in similar circumstances – regardless of whether their income derives from property or wages – bear the same tax burden; and that people in different circumstances bear an "appropriately different burden" based on ability to pay. An understanding that economic power resides in having discretionary income to command resources after the necessities of life of the immediate members of a family are provided for reveals by no means an unsophisticated understanding of a certain dimension of power in society. As for the well-being of those with little discretionary income, no less admirable was the Carter Report's insistence that the necessities of life be defined not as mere physical subsistance, but in terms of appropriate living standards relative to others in one's place and time.

But relations of power are not the same thing as gradations of power. Nor does economic power just command more resources, as conventionally understood in terms of goods and services: it commands other people's capacities. However useful an argument that "a buck is a buck" may be from the point of view of making a case of who is really able and justified to be called on to pay state taxes, the argument that the source of the income is immaterial does not help to clarify how our system works. For the source of certain "bucks" lies in the immense power that some people and corporations have in the economic system, power that the state itself – and, above all, state finance – is dependent upon. By putting its thematic emphasis on horizontal equity in the expectation that it might most easily achieve greater vertical equity under the symbolic cover of a "buck is a buck," the Carter Report made a gamble, which it lost when the inevitable attack was mounted by business and its tax professionals. The tax professionals make the money they do (see where the lawyers and accountants were placed in Pen's parade?) because they are not likely to miss noticing that, under the rubric of horizontal equity, vertical-equity motivations were very much at play in the report (not least Carter's incursions against the hallowed, but never justifiable on pure capitalism's own terms, intergenerational legacies).

Certainly, it is paradoxical that the Carter Report's offer of compromise with capital, entailing a lower overall marginal tax rate in exchange for greater horizontal equity, should have been reincarnated for very different purposes in the 1980s. (And with very different effects: whereas the Mulroney reforms benefited the very richest 1 per cent, the Carter Report's recommendations, if implemented, would have cost the top 1 per cent of income recipients a great deal of money, indeed no less than $67,000 per year for each of those 663 people earning over $300,000 in 1968.) But it reflects a weakness in the Carter Report's approach that the discourse used to justify the 1988 exercise looked similar to their own of 20 years earlier.

It is extremely unfortunate that the theoretical literature on public finance continues to offer so little that might help guide a major project for egalitarian structural reform today. Indeed, the traditional "softness" of this literature in terms of vertical equity,[10] despite its orientation in favour of progressive taxation, may indeed have contributed to the eclipse of vertical equity from theoretical economics in the past few decades, as the ending of the long postwar boom made the trade-off between equity and efficiency more and more difficult to sustain in the real world. As a recent European text (Streissler 1989, 44–5) put it:

> For at least a century before the 1970s economists had regarded progressive taxation mainly from the angle of interpersonal equity and consequently mainly as a question of the redistribution of given incomes ... [But] since the 1970s more and more theoretical authors have questioned the concentration on tax equity as altogether one-sided ... The case for

less progressive taxation of wage income ... has been taken up vigorously from different angles by a number of authors. The theoretical case for less progressive taxation of capital formation is already quite traditional. But it has gained renewed practical importance with the decline in the growth performance of the industrial world during the last fifteen to twenty years.

Distributive Justice in Political Philosophy

Given this development in theoretical economics, the commission may want to turn to political philosophy where discussions of distributive justice have flourished in the last 20 or so years. While it is not possible to take this up here in any properly substantive manner, we may at least draw some pertinent conclusions from the relevant literature.

It is unlikely that the commission will be much tempted by the libertarian defence of the capitalist system of distribution of property and income as inherently and unproblematically just, to the point that no redistribution is itself regarded as just. As Philip Green (1985, 64) puts it in his critique of Robert Nozick: "What is really in question is the extent of the special rewards, if any, deserved by 'economic genius'; and the extent of the special incentives, if any, required by it. We do not reward talented musicians or intellectuals with far-reaching rights of ownership over the activities of thousands or millions of other people, nor do we think that the promise of such rewards is necessary to encourage them to develop those talents."

Nor is the commission likely to be content with returning to the utilitarianism that was the very basis of the "softness" in public-finance theory on vertical equity to begin with. It is difficult to grant that only individual subjective definitions of satisfaction ought to be the basis for moral claims, at least without asking how these preferences are formed and inquiring into what the needs allegedly being satisfied are. In any case, the assumption that marginal utility diminishes with greater economic resources rather than actually growing with income is empirically dubious. Why should society indulge any appetite, no matter how large as long as it continues to remain gargantuan, no matter how much it may be fed? (Shel Silverstein's [1974, 160–1] marvellous children's poem "Hungry Mungry" comes to mind: "He ate the Egypt pyramids and every church in Rome, / And all the grass in Africa and all the ice in Nome. / He ate each hill in green Brazil and then to make things worse / He decided for dessert he'd eat the universe.") Above all, as Amartya Sen (1980, 201–2) puts it: "Insofar as one is concerned with the *distribution* of utilities, it follows immediately that utilitarianism would give one little comfort. Even the minutest gain in total utility *sum* would be taken to outweigh distributional inequalities of the most blatant kind."[11]

Rather more attractive to the commission is likely to be John Rawls's general theory of distributive justice.[12] Rawls turns utilitarianism on its head by justifying inequality only to the extent that it yields efficiency gains, which redound to everyone's advantage (not just enhancing the total sum), with distributional priority given, moreover, to the well-being of the worst off. This well-being is defined not in terms of marginal utilities but in terms of a package of "primary goods" composed of "rights, liberties and opportunities, income and wealth, and the social basis of self-respect," with liberties and rights given priority. However, there is a clear problem with Rawls's approach, which is, in fact, the social-democratic variant of "trickle down" theory ("pour-down" theory?). His justification for incentives in so far as they benefit the worst off may, in fact, not be very different in practical terms from conventional "supply-side" arguments for tax breaks to capitalists which are so often presented in the name of job security or better wages for the workers dependent upon those capitalists. As Macpherson (1985, 12–13) noted:

> [Rawls's] ethical distributive principle does not permit an increase of welfare state redistribution to a point at which "greater taxes interfere so much with economic efficiency that the prospects of the least advantaged in the present generation are no longer improved but begin to decline". The test of economic efficiency is to be applied explicitly in "the competitive economy" and it logically must be a completely market dominated one in which the negative response of entrepreneurs to increases in taxation reduces the productivity of the whole economy. It is the classical model of the competitive capitalist market economy, in which impersonal market forces determine investment and productivity. Thus Rawls's ethical distributive principle does not prevail over, but is overridden by, the capitalist market relations of production.[13]

A growing school of political philosophy has indeed insisted that an egalitarian must want to equalize the resources available to people rather than equalize their welfares. This radical version of equal-opportunity theory, as developed by Dworkin, has been carried further by Roemer (1985) who attempts to show that "the distinction is misconceived, and that the only coherent conception of resource equality implies welfare equality."[14] Sen (1977) goes farther still and invites us to equalize not resources but capacities (thus giving preference to the handicapped in distribution so they can enhance their otherwise more limited satisfactions). He conceives this as possible because, like Macpherson, he insists that egalitarian theory must abandon the norm of the "rational fool": the individual self-interested maximizer. ("The *purely* economic man is indeed close to being a social moron.") He makes a strong case that rational behaviour is social commitment and that people are capable of it, even if its empirical importance may vary.

All these discussions effectively presuppose an egalitarian-democratic alternative to capitalist society, with the kind of behaviour conducive to establishing that alternative being rather different from what we are accustomed to. As Macpherson (1985, 16–17) put it:

> Such a transformed society is unlikely to be achieved by pressures which rely, as trade unions and social democratic parties traditionally have done, mainly on making their case on grounds of distributive justice. By the time such a transformed society was reached, the main concern of the movements which had brought it into being, and which presumably would give it its direction, would no longer be distributive justice. Priority would have been given to other values, which may be summed up as the quality of life: not merely the quality of the physical environment ... but also the quality of the social and economic institutions which would be seen as determining (and hampering) the chances of the full use and development of human capacities.

Iris Young's (1990, 21–3) recent feminist critique of "the distributive paradigm" in contemporary political philosophy has similarly stressed the importance of focusing on transforming the institutional framework within which power relations are constituted and reproduced:

> Discussions of economic justice ... often de-emphasize the decision-making structures which are crucial determinants of economic relations. Economic domination in our society occurs not simply or primarily because some persons have more wealth and income than others, as important as this is. Economic domination derives at least as much from the corporate and legal structures and procedures that give some persons the power to make decisions about investment, employment, interest rates, and wages that affect millions of other people. Not all who make

these decisions are wealthy or even privileged, but the decisionmaking structure operates to reproduce distributive inequality and the unjust constraints on people's lives ... Rarely do theories of justice take such structures as an explicit focus.

From Fair Taxation to Structural Reform

The conclusion this leads us to is clear: it is one thing to come up with a set of proposals for a "fairer" tax system, but quite another to expect that such proposals will be implemented, much less even touch the root causes of economic injustice in our society, given the structures of power and authority within which both the tax system and the existing distribution of income and wealth are embedded. Any serious program for reform has to address this dimension of the problem.

The ignominious defeat of the Carter Report's proposals brought precisely these kinds of questions to the fore for my generation of political scientists and sociologists. It raised a series of questions about whether the state is best conceived (as it always has been in the public-finance literature) as an embodiment of a general interest that transcends the particular interests of capitalist society. Without succumbing to a left-wing variant of vulgar social science, we asked whether the state, even the liberal democratic state, is better conceived as structured by its own history, mode of organization, and financial base to reproduce capitalism's fundamental inequalities. Such a theory of the state may put less emphasis than is common in public-choice or pluralist theory on the direct external influence of business (e.g., wielding its immense and concentrated lobbying resources to defeating the Carter Report plan); it often puts rather more emphasis on the internal goals, assumptions, and organization of key state apparatuses (e.g., the role of the Department of Finance in pushing the Carter Report off the agenda).[15]

To emphasize how the state is structured so as to reinforce inegalitarian social relations is not to say that progressive reforms are impossible. Since power needs to be conceived as relational, albeit asymmetric, this means that there are always non-capitalist social forces capable of mobilizing to try to shift the balance of the "net transfer of powers." Many historical examples of structural reforms achieved in this way may be noted: the right to vote for the non-propertied (workers, women, Natives); freedom of association, the collective-bargaining regime and the right to strike; many facets of the welfare state; recently, equal-pay reform for women. All these involved the coalition of some elements within the state and social forces outside before such changes could be effected. But such reforms, unless they can generate further and more fundamental structural reforms, not least a further democratization of state institutions themselves, are likely to be negated eventually in the face of the continuing logic and dynamic of capitalism. This is what appears to have happenned with progressive taxation.

The generality of the retreat from vertical equity in recent years, extending even to social-democratic governments, suggests that serious investigations of limits and possibilities of fair taxation today need to begin, not by assuming that the cause of the decline in progressive taxation in this country rests only with the ideology and narrow interests of neoconservative politicians in Canada, but rather by searching for more fundamental causes. The most plausible hypothesis to guide such an inquiry would appear to be one that associates this general retreat with the passage from an era of unprecedented economic boom in the first quarter-century after the Second World War to an era of renewed and accelerating economic crisis in the quarter-century that has followed. The guiding principles of the tax regimes that were established by political coalitions in the wake of the Second World War were sustained by the quite exceptional conditions of the immediate postwar decades: i.e., a massive renewal of capital stock after so much capital had been destroyed in the historically unique circumstance of a Great Depression followed by a World War; large pools of cheap labour and raw materials; and clusters of technological innovation bearing fruit in terms of productivity growth and consumer demand.

But these conditions could not last forever. The "golden age" of Western capitalism came to an end in the late 1960s and early 1970s as the special conditions that fuelled it ran their course amid the interrelated contradictions the great boom had generated. Signs of overaccumulation, uneven productivity growth and, above all, a general trend towards declining profitability could increasingly be discerned.[16] We had entered a new era, marked by conditions of increased competition among the advanced capitalist economies and challenges to the stability of the U.S. dollar and fixed exchange rates, on the one hand, and, on the other, by inflationary pressures from trade-union militancy generated under conditions of full employment, and rising commodity prices for Third World resources (dramatized by the 1973 "oil shock"). Neither the political compromises that established the

Keynesian welfare state nor those that established the Bretton Woods system of fixed exchange rates could be sustained in this new context. Macro-economic policies proved incapable of extricating national economies from "stagflation" in these circumstances, while their vulnerability to international financial markets once again became increasingly manifest. In terms of its recognition of the severe contradictions which had come to beset public finance, O'Connor (1973) proved remarkably insightful.

What has been clearly revealed in this context is not only the continued dependence of communities, citizens, and workers on private-investment decisions, but the continued organization of the state in a manner which reinforces that dependence. The structural reforms around welfare and taxation regimes of the postwar era had been constructed through a politics of class compromise which left this fundamental problem for democratic-egalitarian values unresolved. The return of crisis conditions momentarily brought back onto the agenda of a number of social-democratic parties the issue of effective control over private investment, the most famous example of this being the trade-union movement's Wage Earner Fund scheme in Sweden. But neither the ideological nor the institutional ground had been prepared for this by the politics of compromise of the earlier era. As they contemplated possible directions out of the crisis, policy makers took the kinds of readings of the economy that were premised primarily on the need to accommodate to the pattern of investment set in the private sector. The attempt to bribe private capital to invest via regressive tax changes stemmed as much from this as it did from big business seizing the economic policy agenda just by virtue of its rhetorical reassertion of faith in free trade and free markets as the *sine qua non* for renewed economic dynamism.

To be sure, such ideological bravado was not unimportant and had its material underpinnings in the technological revolution in communication introduced by the microchip; by the space which vast flows of international trade and finance opened up for capital mobility; and by the restructuring of conditions of production that simultaneously made it more integrated internationally and more flexible locally in terms of labour and material inputs. Combined with increasingly severe recessionary bouts, the restructuring of industry as a result of the developments noted above resulted in the re-emergence of mass unemployment and a sharp redistribution of power and income away from labour. This has been seen most graphically in the United States where the ratio of the salary of a CEO for one of the hundred largest corporations to the average factory wage, which had stood at 40 to 1 in 1960 (but only 12 to 1 after taxes) stood at 93 to 1 in 1988 (and no less than 70 to 1 after taxes).[17] Where a stronger labour movement had achieved greater weight in relation to the state in the previous era, there were more protracted defences of earlier reforms, but through the course of the 1980s no advanced capitalist state remained immune from quite severe measures of fiscal austerity and regressive changes in taxation.

The irony of this is that it has not led to a new era of stable and sustained capitalist growth. As Clarence Barber (1991, 206) recently pointed out: "During the twenty-five years from 1948 to 1973, world economic output grew in real terms at an annual rate of about 5 per cent, and real capital spending in the OECD group of developed countries grew fairly steadily at a rate of 6 per cent a year. But since 1975 the world growth rate of output has fallen to about 2.5 per cent and there has been almost no growth in the level of capital spending." After the artificial boom of the mid-1980s, the 1990s opened with a severe recession that, unlike the one that greeted the 1980s, was not strategically planned. The current recession has proven to be as general in its spatial and industrial reach (from California to Germany to Japan, from automobiles to computers to financial services) as was the shift towards regressive taxation itself. The alleged "efficiency" grounds for broad tax incentives to private capitalist investment, the alleged economic "rationality" of such private-investment decisions, stand in the shadow of today's empty office towers. Hard on the heels of the banks' unwise loans to Latin American military dictators abroad followed their equally unwise loans to fuel the speculative property and merger boom at home. Meanwhile, the interest on the public debt that weighs so heavily as a component of fiscal deficits is being paid out today to many of those very people and institutions whose taxes had been reduced in the general shift away from vertical tax equity and who then lent some of the money saved in taxes to governments. Governments are now paying interest for having had to borrow the very money they used to tax in the first place!

This is where the Fair Tax Commission comes in today. It is faced with the difficult task of outlining a path to a new era of reform that transcends the structural limits the era of progressive taxation ran up against. The old framework of progressive tax reform, marked by its search for the ever-elusive balance between market efficiency and distributive justice, has been cast aside, but it is already clear that the path adopted over the past decade is hardly the best way to move forward. The shift to a more unjust tax structure has already proved not to be efficient: the increased inequality of the last decade was accompanied by a great many unwise and unaccountable economic decisions, and the consequences of these are being visited upon us today in terms of declining growth and productivity rates; in terms of unemployment, hunger, and homelessness; as well as in terms of public-expenditure restraints on social and physical infrastructure, precisely at the moment when such expenditures are most needed.

If there is a lesson to be learned from this it is that new models for tax reform ought not to assume that the unequal system of distribution of market capitalism is the *sine qua non* of economic efficiency. Indeed, the kind of structural reforms that are needed will be those that seek to establish new criteria of efficiency which not only are more socially substantive but offer longer-term measures than was the case in the earlier era of reform, let alone in the reactionary era that has succeeded it. Two sharply contrasting models of reform may be offered to make the distinction clear. University of Toronto political philosopher Joe Carens (1981) advanced a model whereby everyone would be encouraged to earn as much pre-tax income as possible in order to achieve the optimum market allocation of skills and resources, but, at the same time, everyone would be socialized from childhood to accept a tax system so progressive as to distribute annual after-tax income for consumption equally. Such a model not only puts inordinate stress on the power of socialization but also grants far too much to the alleged efficiency of pure market distributions. A rather more useful model, which employs the tax system actually to establish rational social criteria of efficiency and to provide incentives to meet them, has been advanced by Philip Green (1985, 243 ff.). He calls for a system of "social cost accounting" whereby all the external and internal public costs of each business enterprise (from the costs of toxified environmental clean up to the costs to the health budget in treating job-related illness to the welfare costs of maintaining laid-off employees) would have to be accounted for on the company books. This would lay the basis for a more accurate measure of the real cost of commodities than currently is revealed in market prices, with the tax system being reorganized to provide incentives to firms to minimize the social costs of production and of unemployment. In so far as Green would require the company books to be "completely open to the representatives either of interested groups from among the public or of the workers themselves," this structural reform is designed to enhance democratic capacities as well as socio-economic justice and efficiency.

These examples are merely illustrative. It does not fall within the scope of this paper to advance specific tax proposals. Nor could such proposals be seriously advanced unless they strategically addressed the question of how to change power relations, domestically and internationally, whether those are located in the capacity to mobilize and move capital on Bay Street (and on Wall Street), or in the decision-making structure of the Ontario Treasury (and of the U.S. Treasury). One thing is perfectly clear – the viability of whatever specific recommendations for tax reform are advanced by the commission can be gauged only in relation to its capacity to transcend the limits that earlier stages of reform encountered, here and elsewhere.

In so far as the key asset that human beings have to effect change is their capacity for understanding their life world, the commission should see its role not only as offering policy advice to the government, but as educating the public and thereby enhancing the capacity of popular forces to mobilize for progressive structural change, bearing in mind that, even if such change cannot come today, it may yet come tomorrow. The commission can play this role as long as it does not obfuscate the inefficiency as well as the injustice of the retreat from vertical equity, and produces a report that actually explains in popular terms (to recall the quote from Schumpeter at the beginning of this paper) how "the kind and level" of inegalitarian tax structure we have arrived at today was indeed "determined by the social structure" of inegalitarian class relations that was left in place by the earlier era of reform. This would lay the basis for the identification of those structural reforms in the tax system – including reforms in the structure of the state and in its relation to the economy – which are necessary if we want to contribute, not just to greater post-tax distributive justice, but to transcending those inegalitarian class relations. Such a report by the commission would stand as a vital expression of those social forces in Canada and elsewhere that are oriented towards realizing democratic egalitarian values. The real challenge before the Fair Tax Commission, in other words, is to prove that it can be, in Schumpeter's words, "a handle ... which social powers can grip in order to change the structure."

Notes

The first draft of this study was prepared for the Ontario Fair Tax Commission and completed in February 1992.

1 Quoted in Webley et al. (1991, 1)
2 Cronin and Radtke (1987, 291–2). Cf. Therborn (1977); Bates (1991); and Krever (1981)
3 Messere (1988, 287). All the articles in this volume (covering 11 of the 18 OECD countries) provide a useful guide to the generality of the trend identified here.
4 For evidence on proportionality at best in Canada, see Gillespie (1980). For the United States, see Pechman (1985).
5 Phillips (1990, 1) writes here of the Republican Party, but similar observations, no less astute as regards the parties of business in Canada and the United Kingdom, could have been drawn from McQuaig (1987) and Rentoul (1987). These excellent books, each by popular writers who make their living in the media, eclipse most studies produced in the halls of academe on recent tax policy, especially by demonstrating venal concerns in decision making and their inegalitarian effects with a degree of clarity uncapturable by Gini coefficients and Lorenz curves.
6 In so far as the concept of fair taxes might be used to refer to some standard internal to the state that makes the imposition of taxes procedurally correct in the sense of non-arbitrary action under the rule of law, then we are in the juridical realm where legal or constitutional usage is more common and appropriate. When the Carter Report defended the decision to give the principle of fair taxes greatest weight in its report partly because the state might otherwise be considered justified in arbitrarily commandeering resources from those who "happened to be in easy reach of the state," the report may have been hinting at a very important point about the distribution of power in society in relation to who is more or less capable of resisting the state, but it was being somewhat disingenuous in not distinguishing between juridical and equity dimensions of the issue. In so far as we want to contemplate whether it is legitimate for a state to levy taxes at all, or in what quantity in relation to the nature of its activities, we are more properly in the realm of "no taxation without representation." That is, we require some means of assessing the role and nature of the state in relation to society, a matter which goes far beyond the scope of the

distributional realm intended by the notion of fair taxation. Indeed, a concern often expressed in public-finance literature, to the effect that the state might suffer delegitimation if the burden of taxation is not fairly shared, always begs the question of whether the social and political system deserves to be, as the Carter Report put it, "strong and enduring." For the relevant passages, see Canada, Royal Commission on Taxation (1966, 1: 4 and 2: 17).

7 Quoted in Musgrave (1987, 120)

8 Even though the tax reform of 1988 certainly benefited the top 1 per cent of income recipients (see Maslove 1989), we may nevertheless be appreciative of the measure of redistribution that remains in a system of public finance that, after transfers and taxes, increased in 1989 the share of the bottom two quintiles by over 7 per cent and reduced that of top quintile by almost the same amount. Statistics Canada (1989, Text Table III, 16)

9 See the most comprehensive study of the Carter Report (most undeservedly still not published as a book) by Leslie T. MacDonald (1985), esp. chapter 4.

10 See Musgrave (1987, 114)

11 Nor does so-called "fairness theory" seem to resolve the problem: it defines egalitarianism as a set of distributions in which there is no envy, and then squares the circle with efficiency by designating fairness as the condition which combines Pareto optimality with egalitarianism (no envy). See Varian (1974, 9: 63–91).

12 Leslie Green's paper for the commission, "Concepts of Equity in Taxation," (this volume) commends Rawls to the commission for offering a "more direct and robust justification of redistributive taxation," indeed for making it a "direct requirement of justice itself" (this volume, pp. 100–1). But Green fails to probe just how far Rawls's acceptance of capitalism's social relations and "efficiency criteria" takes him towards leaving society, and especially the working poor, dependent on incentives to investors. Since the income of workers is significantly determined by the profitability of the firm or industry in which they are employed, Rawls's argument could be used to justify skewing the taxation system to the benefit, for instance, of Spadina Avenue clothing manufacturers rather than to the immigrant women who work for them, on the premiss that working in a higher-profit industry rather than in one with such low profit rates would allow room for wage increases that would outstrip government income supplements to the working poor or equal-pay legislation.

13 For a recent defence of Rawls against Macpherson's critique, see Man-
    dle (1991).
14 Cf. Roemer (1986, 751–83).
15 See Maslove (1989) and MacDonald (1985) for such a contrast of inter-
    pretation.
16 The most comprehensive study of the transition is Armstrong, Glyn,
    and Harrison (1991); cf. Marglin and Schor (1990).
17 Reich (1991, 204–5); cf. Bowles et al. (1990).

Bibliography

Armstrong, P., A. Glyn, and J. Harrison. 1991. *Capitalism Since 1945*, 2d
    ed. Cambridge: Basil Blackwell
Barber, Clarence. 1991. "Can We Avoid a Serious Depression in the Near
    Future?" In *Social Democracy without Illusions*, ed. John Richards, Robert
    Cairns, and Larry Pratt, 201–7. Toronto: McClelland and Stewart
Bates, Robert H. 1991. "The Economics of Transitions to Democracy." *PS:
    Political Science and Politics*, 24 (1): 4–10
Bowles, S., David M. Gordon, and Thomas E. Weisskopf. 1990. *After the
    Waste Land: A Democratic Economics for the Year 2000*. New York: M.E.
    Sharpe
Carens, Joe. 1981. *Equality, Moral Incentives and the Market*. Chicago: Uni-
    versity of Chicago Press
Cronin, James, and Terry Radtke. 1987. "The Old and New Politics of
    Taxation." In *Conservatism in Britain and America: Rhetoric and Reality*,
    ed. R. Miliband, L. Panitch, and J. Saville, 263–96. London: The Socialist
    Register
Gillespie, W.I. 1980. *The Redistribution of Income in Canada*. Carleton Li-
    brary no. 124. Toronto: Gage
Green, Philip. 1985. *Retrieving Democracy: In Search of Civic Equality*. To-
    towa, NJ: Rowman & Allenheld
Institute for Fiscal Studies. 1978. *The Structure and Reform of Direct Taxa-
    tion. Report of a Committee chaired by Prof. J.E. Meade* (Meade Report).
    London: Allen and Unwin
Krever, Richard. 1981. "The Origin of Federal Income Taxation in Can-
    ada." *Canadian Taxation*, 3 (4): 170–88
Laughren, Floyd. 1991. "Taxation Issues and Policies for Ontario." *1990
    Conference Report: Report of the Proceedings of the Forty-Second Tax Con-
    ference*, 2:1–2:10. Toronto: Canadian Tax Foundation

MacDonald, Leslie T. 1985. "Taxing Comprehensive Income: Power and Participation in Canadian Politics, 1962–1972." PhD thesis, Carleton University

Macpherson, C.B. 1973. *Democratic Theory: Essays in Retrieval*. Oxford: Clarendon Press

McQuaig, Linda. 1987. *Behind Closed Doors: How the Rich Won Control of Canada's Tax System ... and Ended Up Richer*. Markham: Viking

– 1985. *The Rise and Fall of Economic Justice*. Oxford: Oxford University Press

Mandle, Jon. 1991. "Rawls and the Left." *Socialist Review*, 21 (3–4): 155–68

Marglin, S.A., and J.B. Schor. 1990. *The Golden Age of Capitalism*. Oxford: Clarendon Press

Marx, Karl. 1959. *Capital: A Critique of Political Economy.*, 3 vols. Moscow

Maslove, Allan M. 1989. *Tax Reform in Canada: The Process and Impact*. Halifax: Institute for Research on Public Policy

Meade Report. 1981. *See* Institute for Fiscal Studies

Messere, Kenneth C. 1988. "Overview." *World Tax Reform: A Progress Report*. Brookings Dialogues on Public Policy, ed. Joseph A. Pechman, 277–89. Washington, DC: Brookings Institution

Musgrave, R.A. 1983. "The Nature of Horizontal Equity and the Principle of Broad-Based Taxation: A Friendly Critique." In *Taxation Issues of the 1980s*, ed. J.G. Head, 21–33. Sydney: Australian Tax Research Foundation

– 1987. "Equity Principles in Public Finance." In *The Relevance of Public Finance for Policy-Making*, ed. H.M. van de Kar and B.L. Wolfe, 113–23. Detroit: Wayne State University Press

New Democratic Party. 1989. *Made in Ontario: A Fairer Tax System*. Background Document. Toronto, May

O'Connor, James. 1973. *The Fiscal Crisis of the State*. New York: St Martin's Press

Pechman, J.A. 1985. *Who Paid the Taxes, 1966-1985?* Washington, DC: Brookings Institution

Pen, Jan. 1971. *Income Distribution: Facts, Theories, Policies*, trans. T.S. Preston. New York: Praeger

Phillips, Kevin. 1990. *The Politics of Rich and Poor: Wealth and the American Electorate in the Reagan Aftermath*. New York: Random House

Reich, Robert. 1991. *The Work of Nations*. New York: A.A. Knopf

Rentoul, John. 1987. *The Rich Get Richer: The Growth of Inequality in Britain in the 1980s*. London: Unwin

Roemer, John E. 1985. "Equality of Talent." In *Economics and Philosophy*, vol. 1, 151–88

– 1986. "Equality of Resources Implies Equality of Welfare." *The Quarterly Journal of Economics*, c1 (4): 751–84

Schumpeter, J.A. 1991 [1918]. "The Crisis of the Tax State." In *Joseph A. Schumpeter: The Economics and Sociology of Capitalism*, ed. Richard Swedborg, 99–140. Princeton, NJ: Princeton University Press

Sen, Amartya K. 1977. "Rational Fools: A Critique of the Behavioural Foundations of Economic Theory." *Philosophy and Public Affairs*, 6 (4): 317–44

– 1980. "Equality for What?" In *The Tanner Lectures on Human Values*, ed. S.M. McMurrin, 1: 201–2. Salt Lake City: University of Utah Press and Cambridge: Cambridge University Press

Silverstein, Shel. 1974. *Where the Sidewalk Ends*. New York: Harper and Row

Statistics Canada. 1989. *Income After Tax: Distributions by Size in Canada*. Ottawa: Supply and Services Canada

Streissler, Erich. 1989. "The International Consequences of Less Progressive Taxation." In *The Political Economy of Progressive Taxation*, ed. Dieter Bos and Bernhard Felderer, 43–70. Berlin: Springer-Verlag

Therborn, Goran. 1977. "The Rule of Capital and the Rise of Democracy." *New Left Review*, 103: 3–41

Varian, Hal. 1974. "Equity, Envy and Efficiency." *Journal of Economic Theory*, 9: 63–91

Webley, Paul, Henry Robben, Henk Elffers, and Dick Hessing. 1991. *Tax Evasion: An Experimental Approach*. Cambridge: Cambridge University Press

Young, Iris Marion. 1990. *Justice and the Politics of Difference*. Princeton, NJ: Princeton University Press

Notes on Contributors

John G. Head is Professor in the Department of Economics, Commerce and Management, Monash University, Australia.

Lars Spencer Osberg is Professor in the Department of Economics, Dalhousie University, Halifax.

Leslie Green is Associate Professor at Osgoode Hall Law School and in the Department of Philosophy at York University, Toronto. He is also Director of the Graduate Program in Law at Osgoode Hall.

A. Marguerite Cassin is Assistant Professor in the School of Public Administration, Dalhousie University, Halifax.

Leo Victor Panitch is Professor in the Department of Political Science, York University, Toronto.

Commission Organization

Chair*

Monica Townson

Vice-Chairs

Neil Brooks*
Robert Couzin*

Commissioners

Jayne Berman
William Blundell
Susan Giampietri
Brigitte Kitchen*
Gérard Lafrenière
Fiona Nelson
Satya Poddar*

Executive Director

Hugh Mackenzie

Director of Research

Allan M. Maslove

Assistant Director of Research

Sheila Block

Executive Assistant to Research Program

Moira Hutchinson

Editorial Assistant

Marguerite Martindale

* Member of the Research Subcommittee
** Chair of the Research Subcommittee